A–Z

of

Wool
Embroidery

SEARCH PRESS

Welcome

This book is dedicated to Vic, Judy, Barbara and Ron with love

Me feeding Mary   *Dad and one of his girls*   *Home sweet home*   *Droving days*

Having grown up on a merino sheep stud, producing this book evoked many wonderful moments in my life. I love the smell of a shearing shed, the heady excitement of ram sales, and the sight of a newborn lamb wobbling to its feet moments after birth. I'm overawed by the majesty of a flock of rams standing against the blue of an Australian winter sky, and I am humbled by the serenity that overwhelms you when droving along a dusty road. I'm proud to be an Aussie and grateful for my heritage.

This book takes us from the sheep's back into the world of embroidery. To stitch with such a soft, nurturing thread and watch a work of beauty unfold before your eyes is indeed deeply satisfying. I hope this is the very experience you will derive from using the *A–Z of Wool Embroidery*.

The first section of the book provides you with general information to get you started. Step-by-step photographs and instructions for over fifty different stitches and techniques will teach you all the skills you need. The last section is filled with glorious designs for you to stitch or adapt to suit your own projects. A full-size pattern is supplied for each design. Many of the beautiful photographs scattered throughout the pages are from *Inspirations*, our quarterly embroidery magazine.

Whether you are a novice or an experienced needleworker, I'm sure you will find something within the following pages to gladden your heart.

Happy stitching,

Sue

Sue Gardner, Editor-in-Chief
Country Bumpkin Publications

Contents

General information

Yarns

There is a wonderful array of woollen and wool-type yarns available for your use. Very fine wools, such as DMC broder médicis, allow you to work as intricately as you can with a single strand of stranded silk. The versatile Persian yarns consist of loosely twisted strands. These can be easily divided so you can effortlessly vary the thickness you wish to work with. Gossamer mohairs have a lustre which is irresistible as do the wool and silk blended yarns.

Tapestry wools allow your embroidery to grow quickly. You can achieve exciting effects when you experiment with knitting and rug making yarns.

Each different type of yarn will bring its own unique properties to your work. In the examples below the same motif has been stitched with the same needle, by the same embroiderer.

Needles

Needles are your most important embroidery tool.

Ideally they should be a similar thickness to the yarn being used. The yarn should fill the hole in the fabric made by the needle but not be difficult to pull through.

The most useful needles for wool embroidery are chenille, tapestry and larger crewel needles. These needles all have long, large eyes, making them easier to thread. Their shafts are relatively short in relation to the size of the eye so they are easier to control than needles such as darners.

Because of their blunt tips, tapestry needles are particularly suitable for embroidering on canvas and even-weave fabrics where it is important that the fabric threads are not split.

| DMC 4 ply tapestry wool | Paterna Persian yarn | Appletons 2 ply crewel wool | DMC broder médicis | Marta's Yarns 4 ply wool | Cascade 2 ply crewel wool |

Hints

If you are having difficulty threading the needle, the following may help:

- Moisten the end of the yarn.
- Use a needle with a larger eye.
- Flatten the yarn as much as possible. The eye of a needle is usually long and thin, not round like the yarn.
- Cut a 2–4cm (¾–1¾") long piece of paper which is narrow enough to go through the eye. Fold the paper in half and position the end of the yarn inside the folded paper, against the fold. Push the paper and yarn through the eye of the needle.

Threading a needle

Because wool is so soft and springy it is often more difficult to thread into a needle than threads such as silk and cotton.

1 Fold the end of the yarn over to form a tiny loop.

2 Squeeze the loop between your fingers so it is as flat as possible. Hold the loop as near to the end as possible.

3 Push the eye of the needle onto the loop.

4 Pull the yarn until the loop is completely through.

Beginning and ending off

The way you choose to secure the yarn can vary depending on personal preference, the technique you are using, the fabric and what the finished project will be.

- Working two tiny back stitches is a suitable method for most types of embroidery. It gives a secure, neat finish and does not create a lump on the back of the fabric. When working the second stitch, split the first stitch to make the yarn very secure.

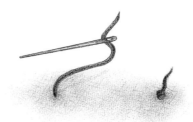

- A waste knot is recommended for beginning in all types of canvas work and can be used in other forms of embroidery as well. Position the knot on the right side of the fabric approximately 5cm (2") away from where the first stitch will be. After working several stitches, cut off the knot and take the yarn to the back.

Rethread the tail into a needle and end off by working two tiny back stitches or by weaving the tail through the back of the previously worked stitches.

Alternatively, position the waste knot so it is in the path of your stitching. As you stitch, the yarn lying on the back of the fabric between the waste knot and your starting position will be secured.

- If you choose to knot the end of the yarn, leave a tail of approximately 1cm (⅜") long beyond the knot. Because wool is springy, a knot too close to the end can often fall out. Once the knot is in position, give it a gentle tug to ensure it will not pull through the fabric.

5

ALGERIAN EYE STITCH

Also known as:
- star eyelet stitch

Algerian eye is a counted thread stitch often used in canvas work. It consists of eight straight stitches, which form a star shape.

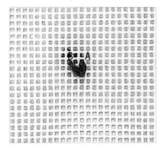

1 Bring the yarn to the front at A, two fabric threads above the centre hole. Take it to the back through the centre.

2 Pull the yarn through tightly to open up the centre hole. Count two fabric threads to the left of A. Bring the yarn to the front in the next hole (B).

3 Pull the yarn through, then take it through the centre hole to form a diagonal stitch.

4 Count two fabric threads to the left of the centre hole. Re-emerge in the next hole (C). Take the yarn to the back through the centre hole and pull through.

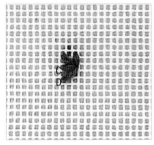

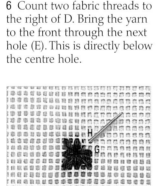

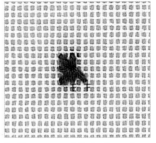

5 Count down two fabric threads from C. Bring the yarn to the front in the next hole (D) and take it to the back through the centre. Pull the yarn through.

6 Count two fabric threads to the right of D. Bring the yarn to the front through the next hole (E). This is directly below the centre hole.

7 Pull the yarn through. Take it to the back through the centre hole and pull through.

8 Count two fabric threads to the right of E and bring the yarn to the front through the next hole (F). Take it to the back through the centre hole and pull through.

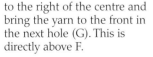

9 Count two fabric threads to the right of the centre and bring the yarn to the front in the next hole (G). This is directly above F.

10 Take the yarn to the back through the centre hole and pull through. Count two fabric threads above G and bring the yarn to the front in the next hole (H).

11 Pull the yarn through. Take the needle to the back through the centre hole.

12 Pull the yarn through. End off on the back of the fabric.

BACK STITCH

Back stitch can be worked by either skimming the needle through the fabric while holding it freely in your hand or by stabbing the needle up and down with the fabric held taut in a hoop or frame.

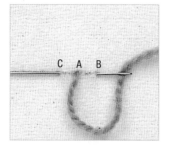

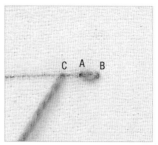

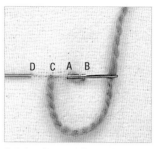

Skimming
1 Mark a line on the fabric. Bring the yarn to the front at A, a short distance from the right hand end of the marked line.

2 Take the needle to the back at B, at the beginning of the marked line. Re-emerge at C. The distance from A to C should be the same as the distance from A to B.

3 Pull the yarn through.

4 Take the needle to the back at A, through the same hole in the fabric. Re-emerge at D. The distance from C to D is the same as from A to C.

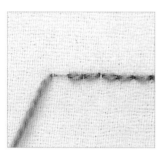

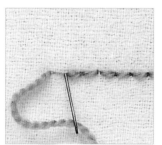

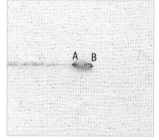

5 Continue working stitches in the same manner, keeping them all the same length.

6 To finish, take the needle to the back of the fabric through the hole at the beginning of the previous stitch. Pull the yarn through and end off.

Stabbing
1 Mark a line on the fabric. Bring the yarn to the front at A, a short distance from the right hand end of the marked line.

2 Take the needle to the back at B, at the beginning of the marked line. Pull the yarn through.

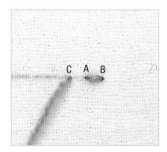

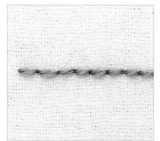

BARGELLO EMBROIDERY

See: Florentine embroidery, page 31.

3 Bring the needle to the front at C and pull the yarn through. The distance from A to C should be the same as the distance from A to B.

4 Continue working stitches in the same manner, keeping them all the same length. Finish, following step 6 above.

BATTLEMENT COUCHING

Battlement couching is a useful filling for simple shapes. It is created from a series of evenly spaced horizontal and vertical straight stitches which are laid down following a particular sequence and then couched with small diagonal stitches.

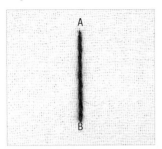

1 **First layer.** Bring the yarn to the front at A and take it to the back at B. Pull the yarn through.

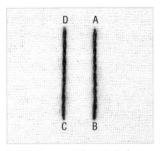

2 Work a straight stitch from C to D, ensuring it is the same length as the first vertical stitch.

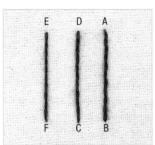

3 Work a straight stitch from E to F. Ensure all three stitches are evenly spaced and parallel.

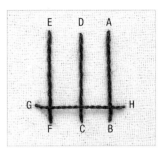

4 Work a horizontal stitch from G to H.

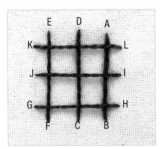

5 Work two more horizontal stitches (I to J and K to L), ensuring the stitches create a grid pattern.

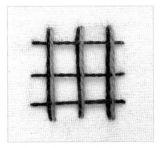

6 **Second layer.** Work a second layer of vertical stitches, positioning a stitch just to the right of each of the first set of vertical stitches.

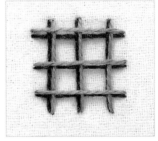

7 Work a second layer of horizontal stitches, positioning each stitch directly above the horizontal stitches of the first layer.

8 **Third layer.** Work a third layer of stitches in the same manner, working the vertical stitches before the horizontal stitches.

9 **Fourth layer.** Work a fourth layer of stitches in the same manner, working the vertical stitches before the horizontal stitches.

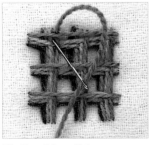

10 **Couching.** Bring yarn to the front, above and to right of one intersection of stitches. Take needle to back over intersection of the two stitches in fourth layer.

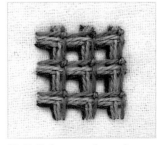

11 Pull the yarn through. Continue working a tiny diagonal stitch in the same manner at each intersection.

12 Alternatively, the diagonal stitches can be worked across all four layers at each intersection.

BERLIN WORK

This form of canvas work originated in Germany about 1804 when a print seller from Berlin, named Philipson, began publishing needlework designs on graph paper. Each square represented a stitch and the tiny symbols within the squares defined the design. By 1810, another Berlin print seller, named Wittich, had begun to produce similar needlework designs. However, each square was hand coloured to indicate the required thread colour.

Tent and cross stitch were the most commonly used stitches, but as the technique developed over time, some pieces included beads and a variety of basic geometric stitches. One particular variation, often known as raised Berlin work or plush work, used areas of velvet stitch among the tent and cross stitches. These areas were trimmed and shaped, giving the finished embroideries a sculpted appearance.

Germany's wool embroidery tradition dates back to the 12th century and German wools were an integral part of Berlin work. The wool of Zephyr merinos was the most sought after. This exceptionally fine wool had no lustre and enabled perfectly even spinning. It produced a very soft yarn, so different from the crewel wools which were available. Zephyr wool was able to take brilliant dyes and with time, came to be produced in fifty colour families, with five shades within each family.

With these sorts of aids, virtually anyone could produce stunning embroideries and so the popularity of Berlin work grew. From about 1830 to 1870 it was so prolific in Europe and America that it displaced almost every other form of embroidery.

Every sort of household item imaginable was decorated with Berlin work – upholstery fabrics, bell pulls, cushions, valances, suspenders, slippers, waistcoats, purses, fire screens, coverlets and the like. The designs themselves were often romantic and sentimental. Colourful bouquets, wreaths and baskets of naturalistic flowers, Shakespearian and biblical scenes, romantic landscapes and whimsical pets were common subjects.

BLANKET STITCH

Traditionally used for edging blankets and rugs, blanket stitch can also be worked as a surface embroidery stitch as well as an edging stitch.

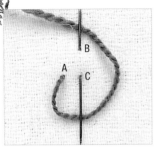

1 Bring the yarn to the front at A. Take the needle to the back at B and re-emerge at C. Ensure the yarn is under the tip of the needle.

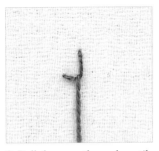

2 Pull the yarn through until it lies snugly against the emerging yarn but does not distort the fabric.

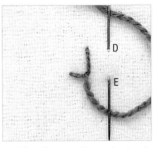

3 Take the needle to the back at D and re-emerge at E. Ensure the yarn lies under the tip of the needle.

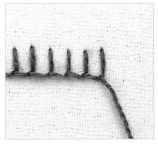

4 Pull the yarn through as before. Continue working stitches in the same manner.

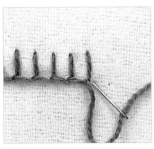

5 To finish, take the needle to the back of the fabric just over the last loop.

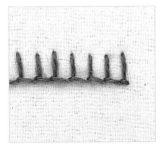

6 Pull the yarn through to form a small straight stitch. End off the yarn.

Butterfly's Day Out, Inspirations 15

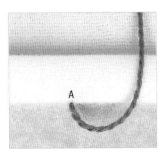

1 **Edging.** Bring the yarn through the fold at A.

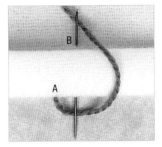

2 Take the needle through the fabric at B. Push it through until the tip appears beyond the fabric edge. Ensure the yarn lies under the tip of the needle.

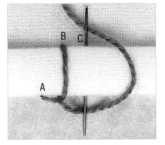

3 Pull the yarn through. Take the needle through the fabric at C. Push through as before. Ensure the yarn lies under the tip of the needle.

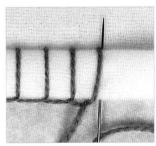

4 Pull yarn through. Continue working stitches as before. After the last stitch, take the needle over the loop and through the fold. Pull through and end off.

BLANKET STITCH – DETACHED

This variation of blanket stitch is worked from left to right on a foundation of straight stitches. The blanket stitches do not go through the fabric.

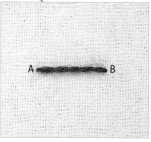

1 Bring the yarn to the front at A. Take the needle to the back at B, the required distance away. Pull the yarn through to form a straight stitch.

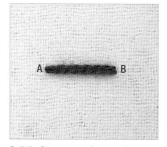

2 Work a second straight stitch from A to B to complete the foundation for the blanket stitches.

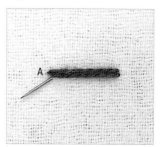

3 Bring the yarn to the front just below A. Pull the yarn through.

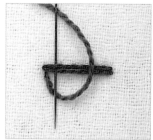

4 Take the needle from top to bottom behind the straight stitches. Do not go through the fabric. Loop the yarn under the tip of the needle.

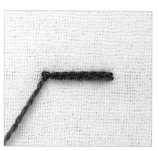

5 Pull the yarn through, pulling it towards you until the stitch wraps around the foundation.

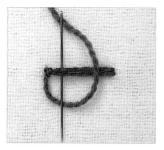

6 Take the needle from top to bottom behind the foundation. Do not go through the fabric. Ensure the yarn is under the tip of the needle.

7 Pull the yarn through ensuring the stitch lies snugly alongside the first one but does not overlap it.

8 Continue working blanket stitches in the same manner until the foundation is completely covered.

9 To finish, take the needle to the back of the fabric just below the end of the foundation.

10 Pull the yarn through and end off on the back of the fabric.

Pansies, Inspirations 20

BLANKET STITCH – LOOPED

The loose tension of this stitch makes it perfect for wool embroidery. The softness and 'spring' of the wool is able to be used to maximum effect. It is wonderful for creating three-dimensional flowers and other motifs.

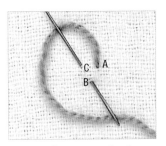

1 Bring the yarn to the front at A. Take the needle to the back at B. Re-emerge at C. Ensure the yarn is under the tip of the needle.

2 Slowly pull the yarn through leaving a loop, which gently rests around the emerging yarn.

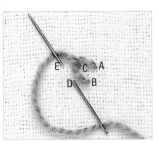

3 Loop the yarn to the right and take the needle from D to E. Ensure the yarn is under the tip of the needle.

4 Pull the yarn through, leaving a loop the same size as the first loop.

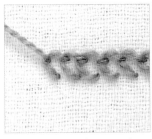

5 Continue working stitches in the same manner, keeping the loops the same size.

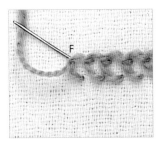

6 To finish, take the needle to the back of the fabric at F.

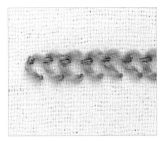

7 Pull the yarn through. End off the yarn on the back of the fabric.

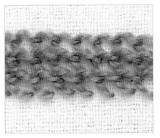

8 To create a textured effect, continue working rows in the same manner allowing the loops of one row to overlap the loops of the previous row.

BLANKET STITCH – PINWHEEL

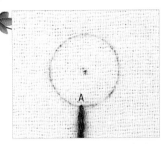

1 Draw a circle and mark the centre. Bring the yarn to the front at A.

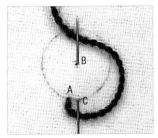

2 Take the needle to the back at B. Re-emerge at C on the edge of the circle. Ensure the yarn is under the needle tip.

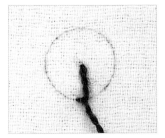

3 Pull the yarn through until it lies snugly against the emerging yarn but does not distort the fabric.

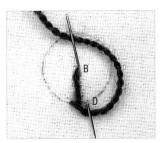

4 Take the needle from B to D. Ensure the yarn is under the tip of the needle.

BLANKET STITCH – PINWHEEL *continued*

Blanket stitch pinwheels and partial pinwheels are an effective way to create flowers.

5 Complete the stitch as before.

6 Continue working stitches around the circle in the same manner, turning the fabric as you go.

7 For the last stitch, take the needle from the centre to A. Ensure the yarn is under the tip of the needle.

8 Pull the yarn through as before. Take the needle to the back just over the loop.

9 Pull the yarn through to form a small straight stitch. End off on the back of the fabric.

Partial pinwheel
1 Bring the yarn to the front at A. Take the needle from A to B. Loop the yarn under the tip of the needle.

2 Pull the yarn through until it lies snugly against the emerging yarn but does not distort the fabric.

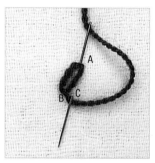

3 Take the needle from A to C. Ensure the yarn is under the tip of the needle.

4 Pull the yarn through as before.

5 Continue to work stitches in the same manner. Begin each one at A and fan them at the outer edge.

6 To finish, take the needle to the back of the fabric just over the last loop.

7 Pull the yarn through to form a small straight stitch. End off on the back of the fabric.

BLANKET STITCH – TWISTED DETACHED

This stitch is a variation of detached blanket stitch and is worked in a similar manner.

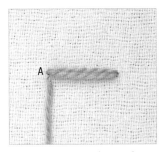

1 Work two straight stitches for the foundation following steps 1 and 2 for detached blanket stitch. Bring the yarn to the front just below A. Pull the yarn through.

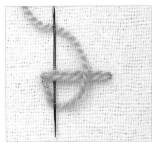

2 Take the needle from top to bottom behind the straight stitches. Do not go through the fabric. Loop the yarn under the tip of the needle.

3 Pull the yarn through, pulling it towards you until the stitch wraps around the foundation.

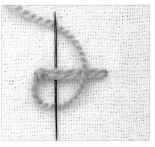

4 Again, take the needle from top to bottom behind the foundation without going through the fabric. Ensure the yarn is under the tip of the needle.

5 Pull the yarn through ensuring the stitch lies snugly alongside the first stitch but does not overlap it.

6 Continue working blanket stitches in the same manner until approximately half of the foundation is covered.

7 Take the needle behind the foundation as before. Ensure the yarn is under the tip of the needle.

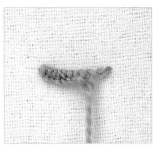

8 Start to pull the yarn towards you until the loop begins to close around the foundation.

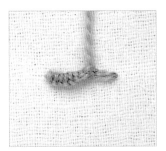

9 Take the yarn up and away from you. Pull in this direction until the stitch wraps snugly around the foundation.

10 Continue to work stitches, following steps 8–11, until the foundation is completely covered.

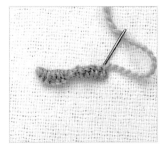

11 Take the needle to the back of the fabric just above the end of the foundation to finish.

12 Pull the yarn through. End off on the back of the fabric.

BRICK AND CROSS FILLING

This filling stitch can be worked on both plain and even weave fabrics. Different looks can be achieved by varying the number of stitches in the satin stitch blocks, using vertical or horizontal satin stitches and by anchoring the cross stitches.

1 **Bricks.** Bring the yarn to the front at A, in the top left hand corner. Take the needle to the back at B a short distance away.

2 Pull the yarn through. Continue working satin stitches of the same length directly below until a square is formed.

3 Alternating with spaces of the same size, work blocks of satin stitch in the same manner.

4 Continue working blocks of satin stitches, forming a chequerboard pattern.

5 **Crosses.** Bring the yarn to the front at C in the lower left hand corner of a space.

6 Take the needle to the back in the upper right hand corner and pull the yarn through.

7 Re-emerge in the upper left hand corner and pull the yarn through.

8 Take the yarn to the back in the lower right hand corner. Pull through to complete the cross stitch.

9 Continue working cross stitches in each space in the same manner.

10 Alternatively, work a cross stitch as before but bring the needle to the front at the centre after working the second diagonal stitch.

11 Pull the yarn through. Take the needle to the back just over the intersection of the two diagonal stitches.

12 Pull the yarn through. Work the remaining cross stitches in the same manner.

BULLION KNOT

The distance between A and B is the length of the finished bullion knot. To form a straight knot the number of wraps must cover this distance. Add an extra 1–2 wraps to ensure they are tightly packed.

↑ indicates top of fabric

1 Bring the needle to the front at A. Pull the yarn through.

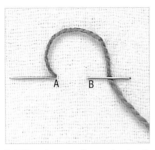

2 Take the needle to the back at B. Re-emerge at A, taking care not to split the yarn.

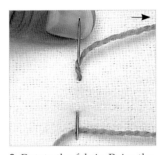

3 Rotate the fabric. Raise the point of the needle away from the fabric. Wrap the yarn clockwise around the needle.

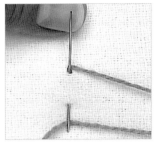

4 Keeping the point of the needle raised, pull the wrap firmly down onto the fabric.

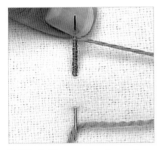

5 Work the required number of wraps around the needle, packing them down evenly as you wrap. The wraps touch each other but do not overlap.

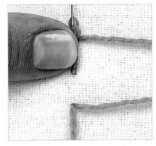

6 Keeping tension on the wraps with your thumb, begin to ease the needle through the fabric and wraps.

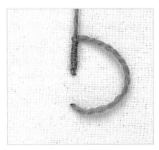

7 Continuing to keep tension on the wraps, pull the needle and yarn through the wraps (thumb not shown).

8 Pull the yarn all the way through, tugging it away from you until a small pleat forms in the fabric. This helps to ensure a tight even knot.

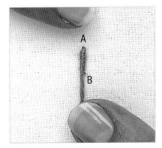

9 Release the yarn. Smooth out the fabric and the knot will lay back towards B.

10 To ensure all the wraps are even, gently stroke and manipulate them with the needle while maintaining the tension on the yarn.

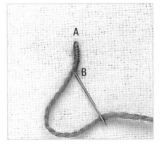

11 Take the needle to the back at B to anchor the knot.

12 Pull the yarn through and end off on the back of the fabric.

BULLION KNOT – LOOP

A bullion loop is a variation of a bullion knot. It is formed in a similar manner, except that the distance between A and B is very short and the number of wraps is often large.

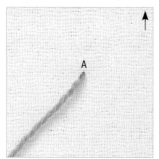

1 Bring the needle to the front at A. Pull the yarn through.

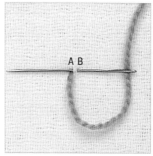

2 Take the needle through the fabric from B to A, taking care not to split the yarn. The yarn is below the needle.

indicates top of fabric

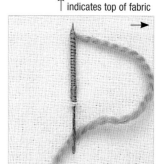

3 Rotate the fabric. Raise the point of the needle and wrap the yarn around it following steps 3–5 for the bullion knot.

4 Holding the wraps firmly with your finger, begin to pull the needle and yarn through the wraps.

5 Pull the yarn all the way through. Using the needle, separate the wraps from the adjacent yarn.

6 Hold the wraps against the fabric with your thumb. Pull the yarn towards you to tighten the wraps and curl them into a loop (thumb not shown).

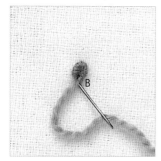

7 Take the needle to the back at B to anchor the loop.

8 Pull the yarn through. End off on the back of the fabric.

Fabrics for wool embroidery

Almost any fabric may be used for wool embroidery and today there are so many to choose from. Embroidery techniques such as the various types of canvas work do require a particular fabric but this does not mean you cannot experiment with those stitches on other fabrics.

Very lightweight fabrics may not be able to support the weight of wool embroidery and very tightly woven fabrics will wear the yarn more quickly than those with a slightly looser weave. Apart from considering these requirements the most important consideration is the type of project you intend to create and what its use will be as a finished piece. This factor should also be considered when deciding what stitches you will use.

When caring for your finished project, both the properties of the fabric and the yarns used need to be considered so it is often easier to use a fabric that has the same care requirements as the yarn.

BULLION KNOT – ROSE

This classic bullion rose uses three shades of pink yarn. The centre is formed with a bullion loop and each inner petal is a half circle.

↑ indicates top of fabric

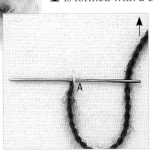

1 **Centre.** Begin with the darkest shade. Anchor the yarn and bring it to the front at A. Take a tiny stitch very close to A, leaving the needle in the fabric.

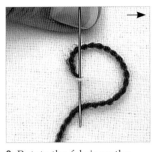

2 Rotate the fabric so the needle faces upwards and away from you. Raise the tip of the needle off the fabric. Take the yarn under the needle.

3 Wrap the yarn evenly around the needle ten times in a clockwise direction. Ensure the wraps lie close together.

4 Placing your thumb on the wraps to hold them firmly, begin to ease the eye of the needle through the wraps.

5 Pull the yarn all the way through. Use the tip of the needle to separate the wraps from the adjacent yarn.

6 Hold the loop on the fabric with your thumb and pull the yarn firmly. Remove your thumb and release the tension on the yarn.

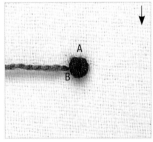

7 Take needle to back at A. End off. **Inner petals.** Rotate fabric. Using the medium shade, bring needle to the front at B, halfway along one side of the loop.

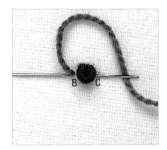

8 Take the needle from C to B, leaving it in the fabric.

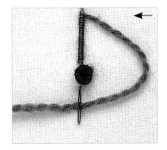

9 Rotate the fabric. Wrap the yarn clockwise around the needle 10–12 times.

10 With your thumb over the wraps, pull the yarn through the wraps. Pull tightly until the fabric forms a pleat.

11 Release the tension on the yarn. Smooth out the fabric. This will cause the stitch to fall into position.

12 Take the needle to the back at C.

Bullion roses can be created in many different ways. However, the overlapping of the knots is common to all variations.

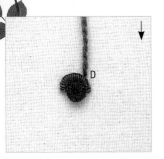

13 Pull the yarn through. Rotate the fabric and re-emerge at D.

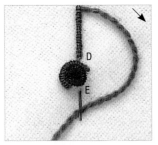

14 Rotate the fabric. Take the needle from E to D. Rotate so the needle points away from you. Wrap the yarn around the needle 10–12 times.

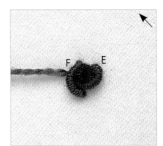

15 Pull the yarn through. Take the needle to the back at E to complete the second petal. Rotate the fabric. Bring the thread to the front at F.

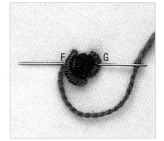

16 Take the needle from G (between the centre and first petal) to F.

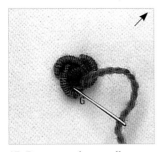

17 Rotate so the needle points away from you. Wrap 10–12 times and pull the yarn through. Take the needle to the back at G.

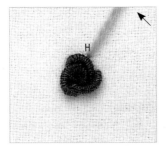

18 End off on the back. **Outer petals.** Rotate the fabric. Change to the lightest shade and bring the yarn to the front at H.

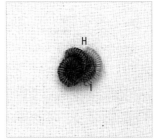

19 Take the needle from I to H. Rotate and wrap the yarn 12–14 times. Complete the bullion knot as before.

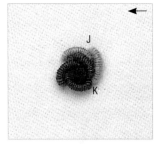

20 Rotate the fabric. Bring the needle to the front at J. Rotate and work a 12–14 wrap bullion knot from K to J.

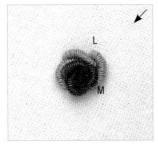

21 Rotate the fabric. Bring the needle to the front at L. Rotate and work a 12–14 wrap bullion knot from M to L.

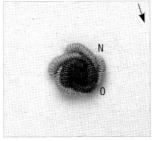

22 Rotate the fabric. Bring the needle to the front at N. Rotate and work a 12–14 wrap bullion knot from O to N.

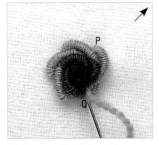

23 Rotate the fabric. Bring the needle to the front at P. Rotate and work a 12–14 wrap bullion knot from Q to P. Q is just inside the first bullion knot of this round.

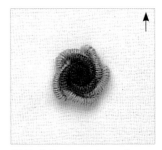

24 Pull the yarn through and end off on the back of the fabric.

CANVAS WORK

Canvas work is such an all-encompassing term. It can be worked with a huge range of threads, not just wool. There are so many types of embroidery which slot into this category, including Berlin work, needlepoint, petit point, gros point, Bargello embroidery and Florentine work. The defining characteristic of canvas work is the type of fabric the embroidery is stitched upon. The fabric, or canvas, consists of crosswise and lengthwise threads, which form a very accurate open grid. It is often made of stiffened cotton but can also be made of silk or linen.

Today, canvas comes in two basic types: mono or single evenweave canvas and double or Penelope canvas. All canvas is available in different gauges or counts, which are determined by the number of threads that cover 1 inch (2.5cm). The higher the count, the finer the canvas.

Although a variety of threads are suitable for canvas work, wool is the most commonly used as it is such a strong, durable fibre. The most popular canvas work stitches are tent stitch and cross stitch. Today there are more than 200 different stitches from which to select and most of them are very easy to work despite their often complex appearance.

Canvas work has a history dating back to the 15th century and one that visits almost every region of the world. During the 16th and 17th centuries in Europe, canvas work was often used to recreate woven wall hangings and carpets. In Japan, Rozashi needlepoint was traditionally used to decorate household items. Today canvas work is still manufactured in factories in China.

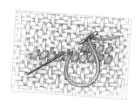

CHAIN STITCH

Chain stitch is a very versatile stitch. It can be used as an outline or a filling and for curves or straight lines. Take care not to pull the loops too tight as they will lose their rounded shape.

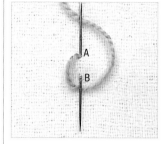

1 Bring the yarn to the front at A. Take the needle from A to B, using the same hole in the fabric at A. Loop the yarn under the tip of the needle.

2 Pull the yarn through until the loop lies snugly around the emerging yarn.

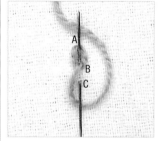

3 Take the needle through the same hole in the fabric at B and re-emerge at C. Ensure the yarn is under the tip of the needle.

4 Pull the yarn through as before. Continue working stitches in the same manner for the required distance.

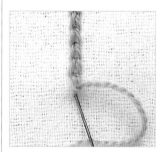

5 To finish, work the last stitch and take the needle to the back of the fabric just over the loop.

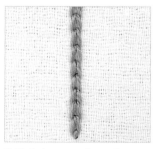

6 Pull the yarn through to form a short straight stitch. End off the yarn on the back of the fabric.

CLOUD FILLING STITCH

This stitch creates a light, lacy filling for shapes. The spacing between the foundation stitches should always be consistent. Use a tapestry needle for the lacing to avoid splitting the foundation.

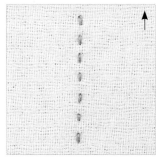

1 **Foundation.** Work a vertical line of short running stitches, ensuring they are evenly spaced.

2 Work a second line of running stitch parallel to the first, ensuring the stitches align with the spaces in the first row.

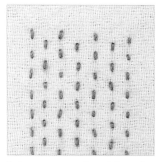

3 Repeat steps 1 and 2 until the required area is filled.

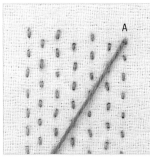

4 **Lacing.** Use a new length of yarn and a tapestry needle. Bring the yarn to the front under the upper right hand running stitch (A).

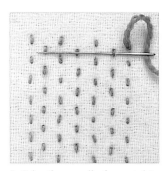

5 Take the needle from right to left behind the next stitch to the left. Do not go through the fabric.

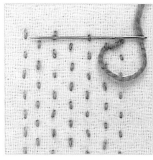

6 Pull the yarn through. Take the needle from right to left behind the next stitch to the left. Do not go through the fabric.

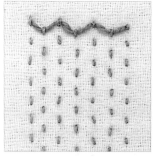

7 Pull the yarn through. Continue to the end of the row in the same manner. Take the yarn to the back under the last vertical stitch and end off.

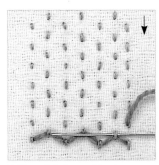

8 Turn fabric upside down. Bring yarn to front under the running stitch above. Take needle behind next stitch to the left. This stitch is shared with first row of lacing.

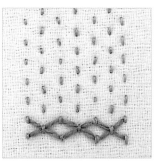

9 Pull the yarn through. Continue across the row as before, ensuring that every second running stitch is shared by two rows of lacing.

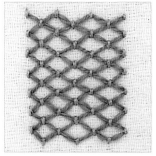

10 Continue working rows in the same manner until the desired shape is filled.

Fruits of the Hedgerow,
Inspirations 8

COLONIAL KNOT

Also known as:

• candlewicking knot

These knots are most commonly stitched close together to form the lines within a candlewicking design. They are similar in appearance to French knots.

1 Secure the yarn on the back of the fabric. Bring it to the front at the desired position for the knot.

2 Hold the yarn loosely to the left. Take the tip of the needle over the yarn.

3 Hook the needle under the yarn where it emerges from the fabric.

4 Take the yarn over the tip of the needle. Shorten the loop around the needle.

5 Take the yarn under the tip of the needle. The yarn almost forms a figure eight around the needle.

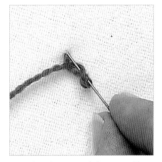

6 Take the tip of the needle to the back of the fabric, 1–2 fabric threads away from where it emerged.

7 Pull the wraps around the needle firmly and down onto the fabric.

8 Keeping the yarn taut, push the needle through to the back of the fabric.

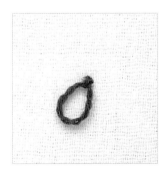

9 Place your thumb over the knot and continue to pull the yarn through (thumb not shown).

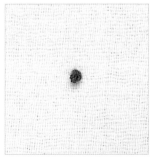

10 Continue pulling the yarn all the way through. End off on the back of the fabric.

Gentle Pursuits, Inspirations 9

22

CORAL STITCH

Also known as:

- beaded stitch, coral knot, German knot stitch, knotted stitch, snail trail

This stitch can be used as an outline or a filling. When using it as a filling, the knots of each row can be aligned or dovetailed with those of the previous row.

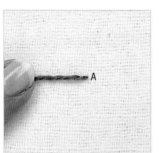

1 Mark a line on the fabric. Bring the yarn to the front at A, on the right hand side of the line. Hold the yarn along the line.

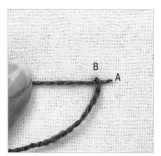

2 Still holding the yarn, take the needle to the back at B, just above the laid yarn. Pull through leaving a loop of yarn on the front.

3 Still holding the yarn, bring the needle to the front at C, just below B and the laid yarn. Ensure the loop of yarn is under the tip of the needle.

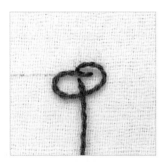

4 Begin to gently pull the yarn through.

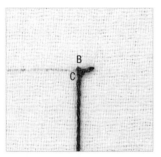

5 Pull until a knot forms between B and C.

6 Lay the yarn along the line again. Take the needle to the back at D.

7 Pull the yarn through leaving a loop on the front. Re-emerge at E just below D and the laid yarn. Ensure the loop is under the tip of the needle.

8 Pull the yarn through to form a second knot.

9 Continue working stitches in the same manner to the end of the line.

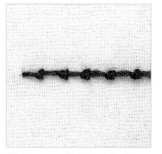

10 You can finish with either a knot or a section of laid yarn. Take the yarn to the back and end off.

Peaches and Cream, Inspirations 5

COUCHING

Couching can be used to work outlines or fill shapes. One to two foundation or laid yarns are secured to the fabric with a second length of yarn and tiny stitches. These stitches hold the laid yarns snugly but do not squeeze them.

1 Bring the foundation yarn to the front and lay it in the desired position on the fabric.

2 Bring the couching yarn to the front just above the laid yarn and near where it emerged from the fabric.

3 Take the needle of the couching yarn over the laid yarn and to the back of the fabric.

4 Pull the yarn through to form the first couching stitch. Re-emerge a short distance away along the laid yarn.

5 Take the couching yarn over the laid yarn and to the back of the fabric as before.

6 Continue working stitches in the same manner to the end of the laid yarn. Take both yarns to the back of the fabric and end off.

Revival, Inspirations 24

Hoops and frames

Hoops and frames are designed to hold the fabric taut while you are stitching. When working stitches that skim through the fabric, i.e. the needle goes in and out of the fabric in one motion, it is best to hold the fabric freely in your hand. Stitches which fall into this category include bullion knots, chain stitch, fly stitch and stem stitch. Stitches that are formed by stabbing the needle up and down through the fabric, such as French knots, straight stitch, split stitch and couching, are best worked in a hoop or frame. Some stitches can be either 'stabbed' or 'skimmed' (e.g. satin stitch) but you will often find that stabbing produces a better result.

• If possible, always use a good quality hoop or frame as these will hold your fabric more firmly and evenly. Hoops that can be tightened with a screwdriver will hold the fabric more firmly than other hoops.

• If stitching on wool blanketing or a similar thick fabric, consider using a quilting hoop. The increased depth of the rings will hold the fabric more firmly.

• Bind the inner ring of a wooden hoop with a cotton bias or woven tape. This will hold the fabric more firmly and be gentler on the fabric.

CRETAN STITCH

Cretan stitch is a filling or border stitch with a plaited appearance along the centre. The stitches can be worked close together or spaced apart.

1 Rule four lines on the fabric to help with stitch placement. Bring the yarn to the front at A, at the top of the first line.

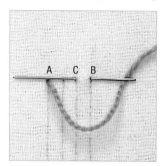

2 Take the needle from B to C. Ensure the yarn is below the needle.

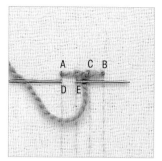

3 Pull the yarn through. Take the needle from D to E. Ensure the yarn is under the tip of the needle.

4 Pull the yarn through until it lies snugly against the emerging yarn.

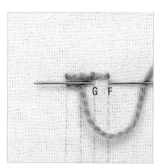

5 Take the needle from F to G. Ensure the yarn is under the tip of the needle.

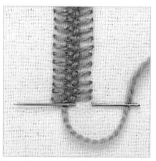

6 Pull the yarn through. Continue working stitches in the same manner alternating from right to left.

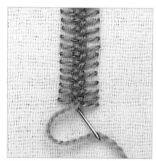

7 To finish, take the needle to the back just below the last stitch very close to where it emerged.

8 Pull the yarn through and end off on the back of the fabric.

Cretan stitch worked within a shape.

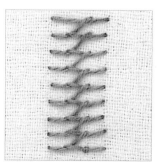

Cretan stitch with the stitches spaced apart.

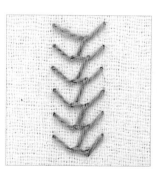

Cretan stitch worked with the needle angled.

Bunny Love, Inspirations 23

25

CREWEL EMBROIDERY

The origins of crewel work are rather cloudy but we can be sure that it has remained a popular form of embroidery for at least four centuries. Examples of linen cloth, embroidered with wool yarn from the 11th century, are still in existence. The most famous is the Bayeux Tapestry which is not a tapestry at all but an embroidery on coarse linen using wool yarn. Believed to have been worked about 1080, the Bayeux Tapestry depicts the conquest of England by William the Conqueror.

The name 'crewel' refers to the type of thread that is used – a two ply worsted wool yarn that is available in a variety of thicknesses and a huge range of colours. The word 'crewel' is thought to have derived from the Anglo-Saxon 'cleow', meaning a ball of yarn.

Crewel embroidery is often called Jacobean embroidery, a reference to the flowing motifs that were employed in crewel work during this period in history. These motifs remained popular and are still common in traditional crewel designs. Many of these beautiful designs, such as the 'Tree of Life', have their origins in India. After the East India company began to trade in the 16th century, there was a steady exchange of design ideas. As England had already established links with China, there was also a strong influence from the fashion for Chinoiserie. The exotic flowers, fruits, animals and birds seen in Jacobean designs are evidence of this cultural melting pot.

Crewel work was most commonly used for dressing beds. Houses were cold and draughty, so a four-poster (tester) bed would be hung with heavily embroidered curtains. A matching valance and bedspread would complete the set. Other common uses for crewel work were wallhangings, pockets and petticoats.

With the settlement of America, designs were carried to a new land where they underwent more changes. American women incorporated plants and animals that were common to them and their designs did not often repeat motifs as did their English counterparts. Designs became much lighter and because of the difficulty obtaining supplies, the settlers had to be very economical with their wool. They employed stitches that left very little yarn on the back of the work, such as Roumanian stitch, rather than more 'wasteful' stitches such as satin stitch.

During the 19th century, huge advances occurred as the Industrial Revolution took place. Roller printing was invented and cheap, mass-produced woven fabrics became available. These changes dealt embroidery a huge blow as many people opted for cheap, printed fabrics in preference to expensive, time consuming embroideries.

Despite this, crewel embroidery has survived, both in its beautiful traditional form and as a constantly evolving textile medium.

CROSS STITCH

Cross stitch is most commonly worked on even weave fabrics and is one of the oldest and best known of all embroidery stitches. Here we show cross stitch being worked in two stages.

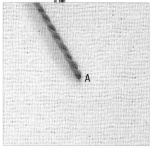

1 First row of half stitches. Secure the yarn on the back of the fabric and bring it to the front at A.

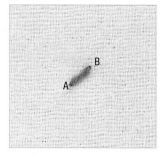

2 Take the needle to the back at B, above and to the right of A. Pull the yarn through.

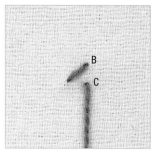

3 Bring the yarn to the front at C, directly below B.

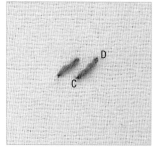

4 Take the needle to the back at D, above and to the right of C. Pull the yarn through to form a diagonal stitch parallel to the first stitch.

5 Continue working half stitches across the row in the same manner.

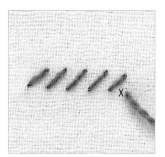

6 Second row of half stitches. Bring the yarn to the front at X where you would stitch if you were continuing the first row of half stitches.

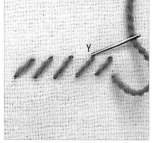

7 Take the needle to the back of the fabric at Y, using the same hole in the fabric as the half stitch of the first row.

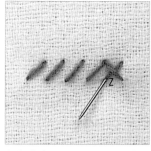

8 Pull the yarn through. Re-emerge at Z, using the same hole in the fabric as the half stitch of the first row.

9 Pull the yarn through. Work a second half stitch following steps 7 and 8.

10 Continue working half stitches across the row, always using the same holes in the fabric as the previous row.

11 For the last stitch, take the needle to the back of the fabric directly above A.

12 Pull the yarn through and end off on the back of the fabric.

DETACHED BACK STITCH

Also known as:
- spider's web stitch

This filling stitch gives the appearance of rows of bullion knots. Work with a loose tension and keep the rows of back stitches packed close together.

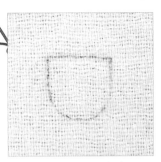

1 **Foundation.** Mark the shape to be filled on the right side of the fabric.

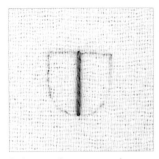

2 Secure the yarn on the back of the fabric. Work a long straight stitch through the centre of the shape.

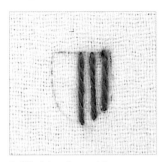

3 Working from this centre stitch, fill one side of the shape with parallel straight stitches no more than 2.5mm (⅛") apart.

4 Fill the other side of the shape in the same manner.

5 **Detached back stitches.** Using a tapestry needle, bring a new length of yarn to the front at the lower edge on the right hand side.

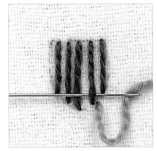

6 Take the needle from right to left under the foundation stitch. Do not go through the fabric.

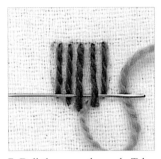

7 Pull the yarn through. Take the needle from right to left under the first two foundation stitches.

8 Pull the yarn through but do not distort the straight stitches.

9 Take the needle from right to left behind the second and third straight stitches.

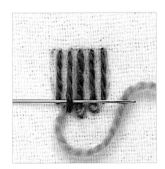

10 Pull the yarn through. Continue in the same manner to the end of the row, always going behind one new and one used straight stitch.

11 At the end of the row, take the needle from right to left behind the last straight stitch.

12 Pull the yarn through. Take the needle to the back of the fabric on the marked outline.

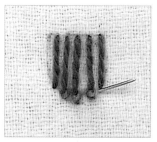

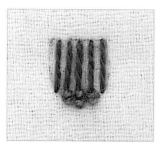

13 Pull the yarn through. Bring the needle to the front on the right hand side of the shape, just above the previous row of back stitches.

14 Pull the yarn through. Work across the row in the same manner as before.

15 Always working in the same direction, continue stitching rows close together.

16 Continue until the entire shape is filled. End off the yarn on the back of the fabric.

DETACHED CHAIN

Also known as:

- lazy daisy stitch

Detached chain can be worked in isolation or in groups. It is often used to create flower petals and leaves.

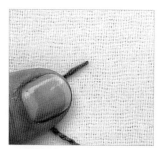

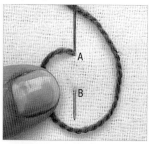

1 Bring the yarn to the front at A, at the base of the stitch.

2 Hold the yarn to the left with your thumb.

3 Take the needle to the back at A and re-emerge at B, at the tip of the stitch.

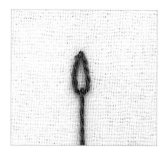

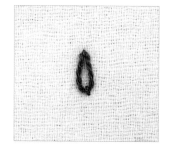

4 Still keeping your thumb over the loop (thumb not shown), pull the yarn through. The tighter you pull, the thinner the stitch will become.

5 To finish, take the needle to the back of the fabric just over the loop.

6 Pull the yarn through to form a small straight stitch and end off on the back of the fabric.

Wool Embroidered Bear, Inspirations 1

ERMINE FILLING STITCH

Created with three straight stitches, the crossed yarns should be further apart at the top than they are at the bottom.

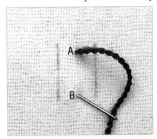

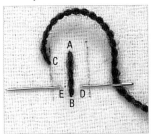

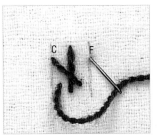

1 Mark two parallel lines on the fabric to help keep the stitches even. Bring the yarn to the front at A. Take the needle to the back at B, directly below.

2 Pull the yarn through. Re-emerge at C. Take the needle through the fabric from right to left (D to E). Ensure D and E are slightly higher than B.

3 Pull the yarn through. Take the needle to the back at F, on the right hand line directly opposite C.

4 Pull the yarn through and end off on the back of the fabric.

FISHBONE STITCH

Fishbone stitch is commonly used for filling shapes and working borders. Stitches are overlapped to give a plaited effect.

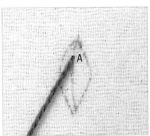

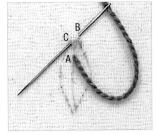

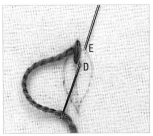

1 Mark the outline of the shape and a centre line on the fabric. Bring the yarn to the front at A on the centre line.

2 Take the needle from B to C. Ensure the yarn is to the right of the needle.

3 Pull the yarn through. Loop the yarn to the left and take the needle from D to E.

4 Pull the yarn through.

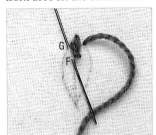

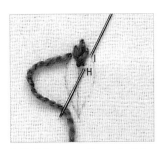

5 Take the needle from F to G.

6 Pull the yarn through. Take the needle from H to I.

7 Pull the yarn through. Continue working stitches in the same manner, alternating from one side to the other.

8 Work the last stitch and take the needle to the back near the centre line. Pull the yarn through and end off.

30

FLORENTINE EMBROIDERY

This form of canvas work is also known as Bargello embroidery, Hungarian point and flame work. It is largely worked as a variation of straight gobelin stitch where the stitches are stepped rather than neatly lined up across the row.

The distinctive designs of Florentine embroidery are based on three traditional patterns: the diamond motif known as the Puzta or feathered carnation; the 'V' motif which is often called Blitz Troellakan, the lightning motif, or thunder and lightning stitch; and the wave motif which is similar to the 'V' motif but is curved rather than jagged.

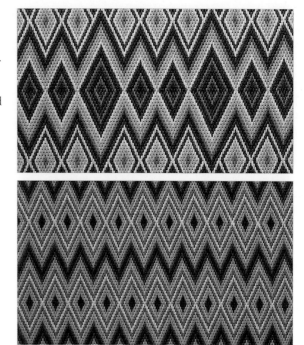

Examples of diamond motif patterns

FLY STITCH

By varying the length of the anchoring stitch and the tension of the yarn, different looks can be achieved.

Also known as:

- open detached stitch

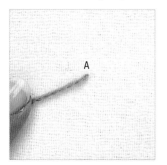   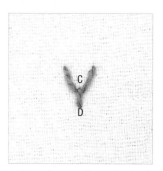

1 Bring the yarn to the front at A. This will be the left side of the stitch. Hold the yarn to the left with your thumb.

2 Take the needle to the back at B and re-emerge at C.

3 Still holding the loop under your thumb (thumb not shown), pull the needle through until the loop lies snugly against C.

4 Take the needle to the back below C. End off the yarn on the back of the fabric.

FLY STITCH LEAVES

These effective leaves are created with several fly stitches worked closely together. They can be made to curl to either the right or the left.

1 Leaf curling to the left.
Bring the yarn to the front at A a short distance from the tip of the leaf. Hold the yarn to the left with your thumb.

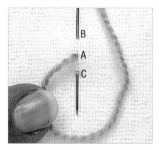

2 Take the needle from B to C. A, B and C are all aligned and B is at the tip of the leaf.

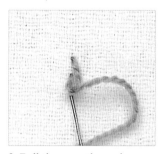

3 Pull the yarn through ensuring it goes under the tip of the needle. Take the needle to the back of the fabric just over the loop of yarn.

4 Pull the yarn through to anchor the loop.

5 Work a second fly stitch around the first.

6 Work 1–3 more fly stitches in the same manner until the leaf is the desired width.

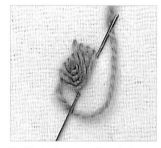

7 Work the next fly stitch directly below the previous stitch. This stitch is the same width as the previous one.

8 Continue working stitches, following step 7, until the leaf is the desired length.

9 End off the last stitch on the back of the fabric. Alternatively, work a smocker's knot (see page 77) at the base of the leaf before ending off the yarn.

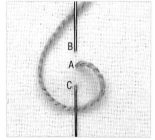

10 Leaf curling to the right. Bring the yarn to the front at A. Hold the yarn to the right with your thumb and take the needle from B to C.

11 Work the stitches in the same manner but as a mirror image of those for the leaf curling to the left.

Rambling Rose, Inspirations Gifts

FRENCH KNOT

French knots can be worked individually or packed close together for quite a striking textural effect. Traditionally they were worked with only one wrap. Today, they are often worked with more wraps.

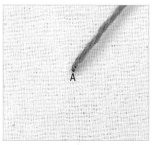

1 Secure the yarn on the back of the fabric and bring it to the front at the position for the knot (A).

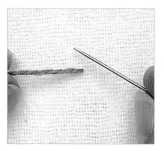

2 Hold the yarn firmly approximately 3cm (1¼") away from the fabric.

3 With the needle pointing away from the fabric, take the yarn over the needle.

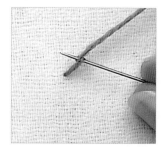

4 Wrap the yarn around the needle. Keeping the yarn taut, turn the tip of the needle towards the fabric.

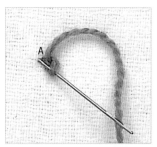

5 Take the tip of the needle to the back of the fabric approximately 1–2 fabric threads away from A.

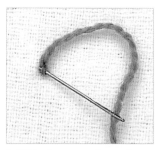

6 Slide the wrap down the needle onto the fabric. Pull the yarn until it is wrapped firmly around the needle.

7 Push the needle to the back of the fabric. Place your thumb over the knot and pull the yarn through.

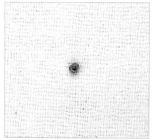

8 Pull until the yarn resists and the knot is firm. End off on the back of the fabric.

GHIORDES KNOT

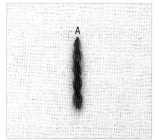

1 **First row.** Take the needle to the back at A on the left hand side. Pull yarn through, leaving a tail on the front of the fabric.

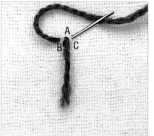

2 Re-emerge at B, just to the left of A. Take the needle to the back at C, just to the right of A.

3 Hold the tail taut and pull the yarn through. Re-emerge at A just below the previous stitch.

4 Pull the yarn through. With the yarn below the needle, take the needle to the back at D.

GHIORDES KNOT *continued*

Also known as:

• turkey work, single knot tufting

The velvety pile is formed by leaving every second stitch as a loop which is later cut and combed. Rows of knots can be worked either away from you or towards you. Here, the rows are worked away from you.

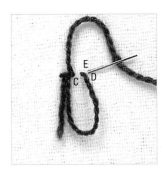

5 Pull the yarn through leaving a loop the same length as the tail. Bring the needle to the front at C and pull through. Take the needle to the back at E.

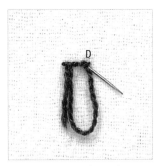

6 Pull the yarn through. Bring the needle to the front at D, just below the previous stitch.

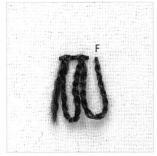

7 Pull the yarn through. With the yarn below the needle, take it to the back at F leaving a loop on the front.

8 Continue to the end of the row. Ensure the last stitch is not a loop. Finish with the yarn on the front. Trim, leaving a tail the same length as the loops.

9 **Second row.** Take the needle to the back of the fabric, directly above A. Pull the yarn through, leaving a tail on the front.

10 Work the second row in the same manner as the first row.

11 Continue working the required number of rows in the same manner. Stand the loops up and trim them evenly. Do not trim them too short.

12 Alternate between combing and trimming until the stitches are the desired height and appearance.

Hints on Ghiordes knots

Ghiordes knot is also a rug-making technique where it is often referred to as rya stitch. The photographs above show the stitches well spaced so the stitch technique is clear. When working an area of Ghiordes knots, you will find that the closer the stitches are to one another, the thicker the plush will be when cut and combed. Ghiordes knots should be worked in straight lines, regardless of the shape that is to be filled. This helps to avoid the stitches becoming tangled in the previously stitched loops. As you work, hold the loops out of the way with your thumb or finger. The direction you choose to fill a shape – top to bottom or vice versa – may depend on the finished effect you require. The lower edge of a row of knots has the securing stitches exposed. When stitching an area such as the guard's bearskin cap in the design on page 108, it is preferable to work from the top of the hat down, so that these stitches are at the base.

GRANITOS

These quick and easy stitches are created by working several straight stitches that use the same holes in the fabric. It is important to ensure the stitches lie alongside each other.

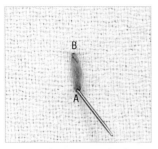

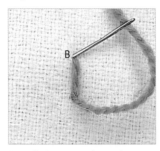

1 Bring the yarn to the front at A. Take the needle to the back at B and pull through. Re-emerge at A, taking care to use exactly the same hole in the fabric.

2 Pull the yarn through. Loop the yarn to the left and take the needle to the back at B.

3 Gently pull the yarn through ensuring the stitch is positioned to the left of the first stitch.

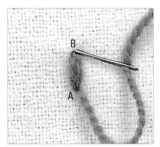

4 Bring the yarn to the front at A and loop it to the right. Take the needle to the back at B.

5 Pull the yarn through with care, placing the stitch to the right of the previous stitches.

6 Work the required number of stitches, alternating them from the left side to the right side. After the last stitch, end off on the back of the fabric.

The Magic Rooster Rug, Inspirations 5

JACOBEAN EMBROIDERY

See: crewel embroidery, page 26.

Woollen or worsted yarns

Wool yarns fall into two main categories – woollen and worsted. Worsted yarns are made from the longer fibres of a fleece. Before spinning, the fibres are combed to remove the shorter fibres and ensure they all lie in the same direction.

Crewel wools are generally made from worsted yarn. Woollen yarns use shorter fibres which are carded, rather than combed, before spinning. The fibres lie in different directions and so more air is held within them. The resulting yarn is softer and has more 'spring'.

LAID WORK

Often seen in crewel embroidery designs, laid work is a useful method for covering large areas. The background is completely covered with satin stitch. A trellis or lattice of laid stitches is then couched to this surface. A large variety of attractive designs and textures can be created.

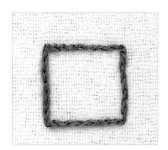

1 **Foundation.** Outline the area to be filled with split stitch.

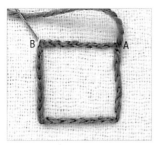

2 Bring the yarn to the front just beyond the outline (A). Work a straight stitch across the shape to the opposite side (B).

3 Continue working satin stitches across the shape until it is filled.

4 **Laid yarns.** Bring a new length of yarn to the front at B. Take the needle to the back at C.

5 Pull the yarn through. Continue working parallel straight stitches across the shape until one half is filled. Keep the stitches evenly spaced.

6 Work the remaining half in the same manner.

7 Work a second layer of straight stitches at right angles to the previous layer.

8 **Couching.** Bring a new length of yarn to the front near one intersection of straight stitches. Take needle to back on opposite side of the intersection.

9 Pull the yarn through. Couch each intersection of straight stitches in the same manner.

Variation of laid work. The couching stitches are worked horizontally; French knots fill the diamond shapes.

Variation of laid work. The straight stitches form a grid and cross stitches are used to couch them in place.

Variation of laid work. A grid of straight stitches is overlaid with diagonal stitches. The intersections are couched in place.

LONG AND SHORT STITCH

This stitch and its variations are known as embroidery stitch, plumage stitch, shading stitch, tapestry shading stitch, brick stitch, leaf stitch, Irish stitch, feather stitch, featherwork and Opus Plumarium. (See also soft shading, page 48.)

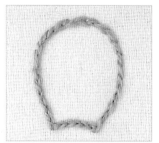

1 Outline the shape to be filled with split stitch. This helps to create a neat edge.

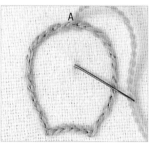

2 **First row.** Bring yarn to the front on the left hand side just beyond the centre top of the outline (A). Take needle to the back of the fabric directly below.

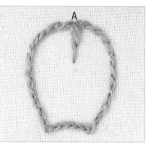

3 Pull the yarn through. Bring the yarn to the front just to the right of A. Work a shorter straight stitch alongside the previous stitch.

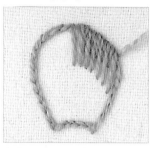

4 Continue working parallel straight stitches across the row in the same manner, alternating a long stitch with a short stitch.

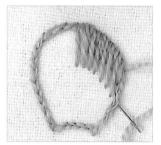

5 Ensure the last stitch goes to the back of the fabric just beyond the outline. Pull the yarn through and end off.

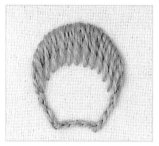

6 Beginning at the centre, work the remaining half of the row in the same manner.

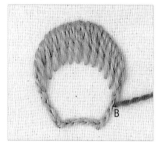

7 **Second row.** Bring a new length of yarn to the front at B. Leave enough distance for this stitch to be the same length as the long stitches in the first row.

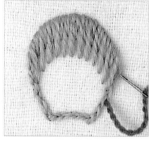

8 Take the needle to the back of the fabric at the base of the first stitch from the right in the first row. This is just beyond the outline.

9 Pull the yarn through. Re-emerge at C to begin the second stitch. This stitch will be the same length as, and parallel to, the previous stitch.

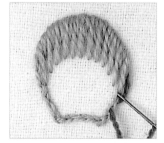

10 Take the needle to the back at the base of the second stitch from the right in the first row.

11 Pull the yarn through. Continue across the row in the same manner and end off. All the stitches are the same length but are staggered.

12 **Subsequent rows.** Work remaining rows, except for the last row, in the same manner. In the last row, the lower end of each stitch just covers the outline.

MOSS STITCH

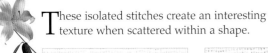

These isolated stitches create an interesting texture when scattered within a shape.

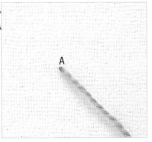

1 Secure the yarn on the back of the fabric and bring it to the front at A.

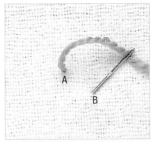

2 Take the needle to the back at B.

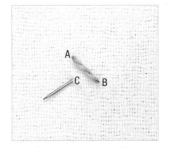

3 Pull the yarn through to form a diagonal straight stitch. Bring the needle to the front at C.

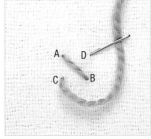

4 Pull the yarn through. Take the needle to the back at D.

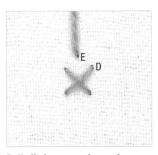

5 Pull the yarn through to form a cross stitch. Bring the yarn to the front at E, above the centre of the cross.

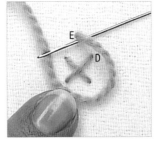

6 Loop the thread to the left. Hold the loop in place and slide the needle from left to right under the yarn between D and E. Do not go through the fabric.

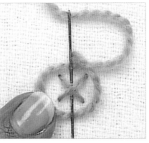

7 Still holding the loop in place, slide the needle from top to bottom behind the centre of the cross. Do not go through the fabric.

8 Ensure the loop is under the tip of the needle. Pull the yarn through until a small loop lies at the centre of the cross.

9 Take the needle to the back at F.

10 Pull the yarn through and end off on the back of the fabric.

Moon Dance, Inspirations 4

NEEDLEPOINT

Often mistakenly called 'tapestry', needlepoint is a type of counted thread embroidery worked on canvas. The canvas can be made from cotton, linen, silk or plastic and varies in size from silk gauze – 46 threads to the inch (2.5cm) – to rug canvas – 4 threads to the inch (2.5cm). As mentioned on page 20, canvas is available in two main types – mono (single thread) and Penelope (double thread). Mono canvas is available with a plain or interlocking weave.

Needlepoint designs can be worked onto unmarked canvas using a pattern, or onto printed or trammed canvas. Tramming is a method of putting the design onto the canvas by working long running stitches in the required colours, parallel to the weft. Needlepoint can be worked in a variety of threads and the most commonly used stitches are those referred to as tent stitches.

OUTLINE STITCH

Outline stitch is very similar in appearance to stem stitch and is worked in a similar manner. However, the yarn is kept above the needle for all stitches.

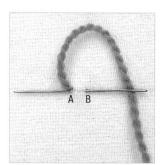

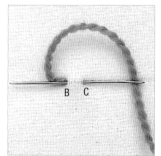

1 Bring the yarn to the front at A on the left hand side. With the yarn above the needle, take the needle from B to A.

2 Pull the yarn through. Again with the yarn above the needle, take the needle from C to B.

3 Pull the yarn through. Continue working stitches in the same manner, keeping them all the same length.

4 For the last stitch, take the yarn to the back but do not re-emerge. End off on the back of the fabric.

PALESTRINA STITCH

Also known as:

• old English knot stitch, double knot stitch, tied coral stitch

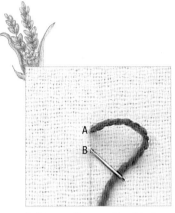

1 Draw a line on the fabric. Bring the needle to the front at the top of the line (A). Take the needle to the back at B.

2 Pull the yarn through. Bring the needle to the front at C, just to the left of B.

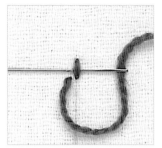

3 Pull the yarn through. Slide the needle from right to left under the first stitch without going through the fabric.

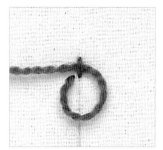

4 Begin to pull the yarn through.

5 Continue pulling until the loop gently hugs the first stitch.

6 Loop the thread to the left.

7 Diagonally slide needle from right to left under the first stitch as shown. Do not go through the fabric. Ensure the loop is under the tip of the needle.

8 Gently pull the yarn through to form a soft knot.

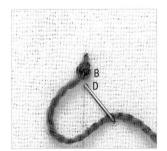

9 Take the needle to the back at D, a short distance below B.

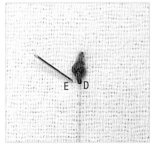

10 Pull the yarn through. Bring the needle to the front at E, just to the left of D.

11 Complete the stitch following steps 3–8.

12 Continue working stitches in the same manner. Take the needle to the back of the fabric close to the base of the last stitch. End off on the back.

POMPOM

Pompoms created in a variety of shades and sizes add a three-dimensional touch.

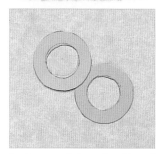

1 Cut two circles of cardboard to the required size of the pompom. Within each circle, cut a second circle so you have two doughnut shapes.

2 Thread a long length of yarn onto a chenille needle. Place the pieces of card together. Take the yarn through the hole and knot it at the outer edge.

3 Take the yarn through the hole again and around the outer edge.

4 Always working in the same direction, continue taking the yarn through the hole so it wraps around the cardboard.

5 To join in a new piece of yarn, knot the new length to the end of the old piece, positioning the knot at the outer edge.

6 Continue wrapping the yarn around the cardboard in the same manner until the hole is firmly packed.

7 Place small sharp scissors between the two pieces of card at the outer edge and cut through the yarn.

8 Cut a length of yarn. Take it between the two pieces of card so it encircles the cut pieces of yarn at the centre. Tie in a firm secure knot.

9 Cut through each piece of cardboard and carefully remove them.

10 Fluff out the cut strands with your fingers to make a ball shape.

11 Carefully trim away any knots or uneven pieces of yarn except for the length used to tie the pompom.

12 The pompom is now ready to use.

ROPE STITCH

Different looks can be achieved with rope stitch by varying the width. Place the needle diagonally when working a wide rope stitch and vertically when working a narrow rope stitch.

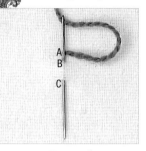

1 Narrow. Draw a line on the fabric. Secure the yarn on the back of the fabric and bring it to the front at the top of the line (A). Take the needle from B to C.

2 Take the yarn from left to right over the needle and then pass it from right to left under the tip of the needle.

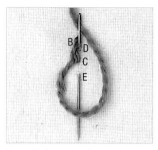

3 Pull the yarn through. Take the needle from D to E. D is just below B and E is below C.

4 Take the yarn from right to left under the tip of the needle.

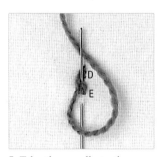

5 Take the needle to the back just below D and re-emerge just below E.

6 Continue working stitches in the same manner for the desired distance

7 To finish, take the needle to the back of the fabric just below the loop of the last stitch.

8 Pull the yarn through and end off on the back of the fabric.

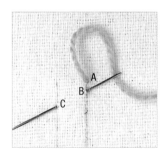

1 Wide. Draw two lines on the fabric. Bring the yarn to the front at A. Take the needle to the back at B, directly below A. Re-emerge at C, below and to the left of B.

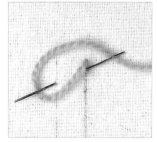

2 Take the yarn from left to right over the needle and then pass it from right to left under the tip of the needle.

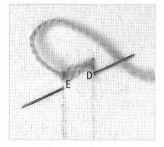

3 Pull the yarn through. Take the needle from D to E. D is just below B and E is below C.

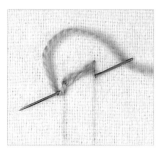

4 Take the yarn from right to left under the tip of the needle.

ROPE STITCH *continued*

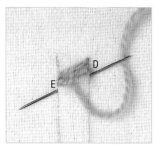

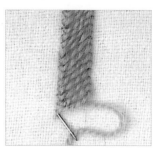

5 Pull the yarn through. Take the needle to the back just below D and re-emerge just below E.

6 Take the yarn under the needle tip and pull through. Continue working stitches in the same manner for the desired distance.

7 To finish, take the needle to the back of the fabric just below the loop of the last stitch.

8 Pull the yarn through and end off on the back of the fabric.

ROSETTE STITCH

Rosette stitch is quick and easy to work. You can create stitches of different sizes by varying the number of wraps and the thickness of the yarn used.

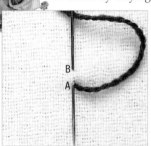

1 Bring the yarn to the front at A. Take the needle from B to A and leave it in the fabric.

2 Pick up the yarn at A. Wrap the yarn under the ends of the needle in an anti-clockwise direction.

3 Continue working wraps in the same manner ensuring they lie side by side rather than on top of each other.

4 Hold the wraps in place with your thumb. Gently pull the needle through.

5 Still holding the wraps in place, take the needle over the wraps and to the back of the fabric.

6 Pull the yarn through. Bring the needle to the front on the opposite side of the wraps.

7 Pull the yarn through. Take the needle to the back just inside the last wrap.

8 Pull the yarn through and end off on the back of the fabric.

ROUMANIAN STITCH

Roumanian stitch can be used to create a broad outline or as a filling.

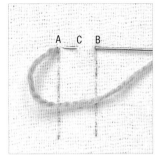

1 Draw two lines on the fabric. Bring the yarn to the front at A. Take the needle from B to C. Ensure the yarn is below the needle.

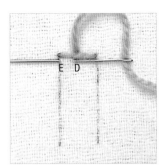

2 Pull the yarn through. With the yarn above the needle, take the needle from D to E.

3 Pull the yarn through.

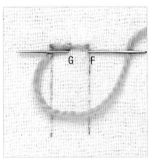

4 Take the needle from F to G. Ensure the yarn is below the needle.

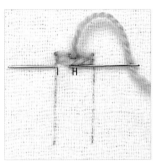

5 Pull the yarn through. With the yarn above the needle, take the needle from H to I.

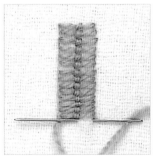

6 Pull the yarn through. Continue working stitches in the same manner.

Why wool shrinks

Wool is an amazing fibre but it can shrink, and once shrunk cannot be returned to its original state. Woollen fibres have thousands of tiny overlapping scales, which all face the same way. Air is trapped between these scales. The outside of a wool fibre repels water but at a certain point of getting wet the inside of the fibre, which is hollow, attracts water. When this happens and heat and the twisting, churning motion of a washing machine are added, the scales move and lock together, and shrinking occurs!

The Woolly Sheep, Inspirations 18

7 To finish, work the first half of the last stitch. Take the needle to the back below the straight stitch but do not re-emerge on the left hand side.

8 Pull the yarn through and end off on the back of the fabric.

RUNNING STITCH

Running stitch is quick and easy to work. It is often used to form the foundation for other stitches. When working on plain weave fabric, make the stitch on the front slightly longer than the stitch on the back.

1 Draw a line on the fabric. Bring the yarn to the front at the right hand end of the line.

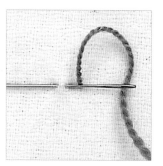

2 Take a small stitch, skimming the needle beneath the fabric along the line.

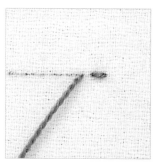

3 Pull the yarn through.

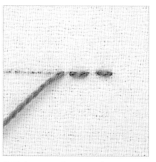

4 Take another stitch in the same manner as before. Ensure it is the same length as the previous stitch.

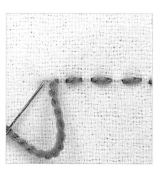

5 Continue working stitches in the same manner to the end of the line. To finish, take needle to the back but do not re-emerge.

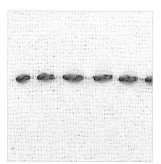

6 Pull the yarn through and end off on the back of the fabric.

Nine Lives, Inspirations 25

Caring for wool embroidery

• Dry clean your embroidery or gently handwash it in warm water using a mild soap or detergent. Gently squeeze to remove excess moisture but do not twist or wring it. Roll the embroidery in a towel to remove more moisture and then lay on a dry towel in a shaded place to dry completely.

• Avoid storing your embroidery in plastic bags. Wool is a natural fibre and needs to breathe. Wrap your pieces in acid-free tissue paper or in another piece of fabric.

• To protect your embroidery from insects, ensure it is perfectly clean before storing it. Use a natural insect repellent such as camphor, cedar or lavender but take care that this does not come into direct contact with your embroidered piece.

• Place items away from direct sunlight or strong artificial light as these will fade your threads and fabric. When framing your work use conservation glass to screen out harmful UV light.

SATIN STITCH

Also known as:

• damask stitch

Work with the fabric in a hoop and angle the needle under the outline when coming to the front or going to the back. When working a curve, fan the stitches on the outer edge and keep them close together on the inner edge.

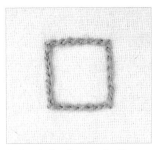

1 **Straight shape.** Outline the shape to be filled with split stitch. This helps to create a neat edge.

2 Bring the yarn to the front at A, just outside the outline.

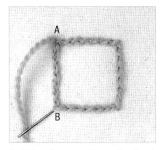

3 Take the needle to the back at B, just over the outline and directly opposite A.

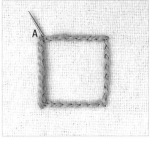

4 Pull the yarn through. Re-emerge next to A, angling the needle from under the outline.

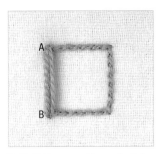

5 Pull the yarn through. Take the needle to the back of the fabric next to B and pull the yarn through.

6 Continue working stitches in the same manner until reaching the end of the shape. End off the yarn on the back of the fabric.

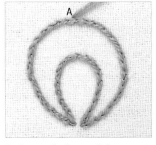

7 **Curved shape.** When working a curved or complex shape, begin near the centre. Bring the yarn to the front at A.

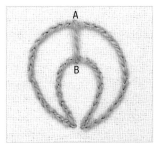

8 Take the needle to the back at B, directly below A. The stitch is at right angles to the shape at this point. Pull the yarn through.

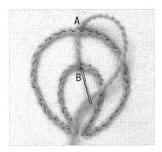

9 Re-emerge close to A and pull the yarn through. Take the needle to the back near B, leaving a slightly narrower space between the stitches.

10 Pull the yarn through to complete the second stitch.

11 Continue working stitches in the same manner, keeping each one at right angles to the outline. When one half is filled, end off the yarn on the back.

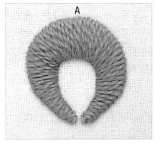

12 Bring the yarn to the front close to A. Fill the remaining half of the shape in the same manner.

SCROLL STITCH

Also known as:

- knotted line stitch

Scroll stitch makes an attractive border. Marking a line on the fabric will help keep the stitches straight.

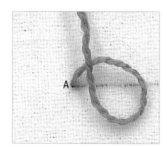

1 Secure the yarn on the back of the fabric and bring it to the front at A. Just to the right of A, loop the yarn in a clockwise direction.

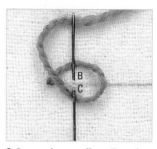

2 Insert the needle at B and re-emerge at C, taking a tiny stitch on the marked line. Ensure the loop of yarn lies under both ends of the needle.

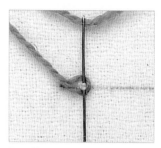

3 Pull the yarn firmly so the loop tightens around the needle.

4 Pull the needle and yarn through to complete the first stitch.

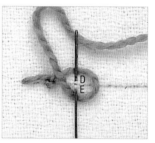

5 Loop the yarn to the right as before. Take the needle from D to E. Ensure the loop is under both ends of the needle.

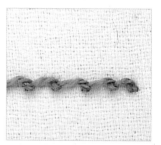

6 Tighten the loop and pull the yarn through. Continue working in the same manner. Take the yarn to the back below the last stitch and end off.

SEED STITCH

Seed stitch is a filling stitch and is sometimes known as speckling stitch or isolated back stitch. When filling an area, the tiny stitches are often randomly spaced and worked at varying angles.

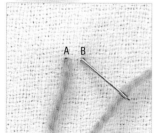

1 Bring the yarn to the front at A. Take the needle to the back at B, a short distance away.

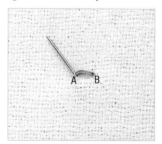

2 Pull the yarn through and re-emerge next to A.

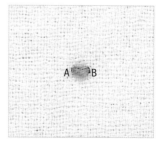

3 Pull the yarn through. Take the needle to the back next to B and pull through.

4 Continue working stitches in the same manner until the required area is filled.

SOFT SHADING

Soft shading is a freer variation of long and short stitch – the stitches are not laid down with the same uniformity and so a very realistic blending of colour is possible.

1 Outline the shape to be filled with split stitch. This helps to create a neat, well defined edge. Bring the yarn to the front at A, just outside the outline.

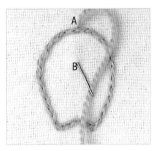

2 Take the needle to the back at B, within the shape.

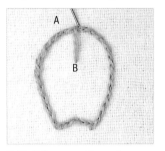

3 Pull the yarn through. Re-emerge just beyond the outline very close to A.

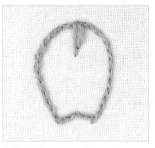

4 Pull the yarn through. Work a second stitch which is slightly shorter than the first stitch.

5 Continue working stitches very close together, fanning them to fit the shape. Alternate between long stitches and shorter stitches.

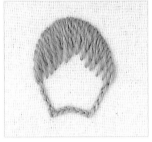

6 When the section is complete, take the yarn to the back of the fabric and end off.

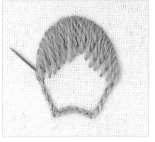

7 Using a darker shade of yarn, bring the needle to the front, splitting a stitch of the previous row.

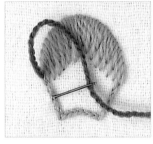

8 Pull the yarn through. Take the needle to the back in the unembroidered area.

9 Work long and short stitches in the same direction as the first row, always emerging through a previous stitch. When complete, end off as before.

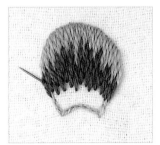

10 Using a darker shade of yarn, bring the needle to the front, splitting a stitch of the previous row.

11 Repeat steps 8 and 9 When complete, end off as before.

Grand Adventure, Inspirations 9

SPIDER WEB ROSE

Weaving the yarn through a framework of straight stitch spokes forms these easy to stitch roses. It is important to have an odd number of spokes. Here, five spokes are used but when working larger roses more spokes are required.

1 Draw a circle on the fabric and mark the centre with a dot. Imagining the circle is a clock, mark the outer edge with dots at 12, 2, 5, 7 and 10 o'clock.

2 **Framework.** Anchor the yarn on the back and bring it to the front at the 12 o'clock mark. Take the needle to the back at the centre.

3 Pull the yarn through. Re-emerge at the 5 o'clock mark and take the yarn to the back at the centre to form a second straight stitch.

4 Work a straight stitch from the 7 o'clock mark to the centre.

5 Work straight stitches from the 2 o'clock and 10 o'clock marks in the same manner.

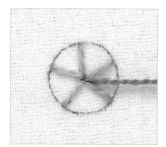

6 **Weaving.** Bring the yarn to the front between two spokes as close as possible to the centre.

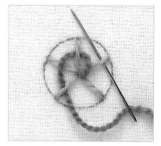

7 Work in an anti-clockwise direction; weave the yarn over and under the spokes until one round is complete.

8 Pull the yarn firmly so the framework does not show through at the centre.

9 Continue weaving the yarn over and under, keeping the rounds close together.

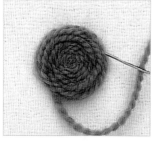

10 Continue until the framework is entirely hidden. Take the needle over one more spoke. Tuck it under the next spoke to take it through to the back.

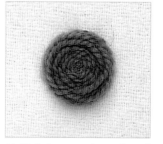

11 Pull the yarn through and end off securely on the back of the fabric.

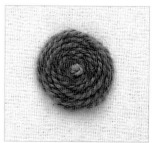

12 **Centre.** Work a French knot at the centre.

SPLIT STITCH

Split stitch was used extensively in the Middle Ages. It can be worked in multiple rows as a filling or used as an outline.

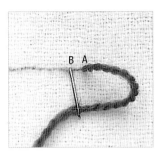

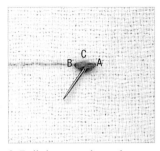

1 Bring the yarn to the front at A on the right hand side. Take the needle to the back at B, a short distance away.

2 Pull the yarn through. Bring the needle to the front at C in the middle of the first stitch, splitting the yarn.

3 Pull the yarn through.

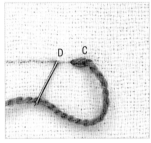

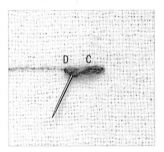

4 Take the needle to the back of the fabric at D. C to D is the same distance as A to B.

5 Pull the yarn through. Re-emerge through the stitch halfway between C and D.

6 Pull the yarn through. Continue in the same manner for the desired distance. End off on the back of the fabric.

SPLIT BACK STITCH

On the front of the fabric, split back stitch looks very much like split stitch. However, each stitch is split when the needle is taken to the back of the fabric rather than when it is emerging.

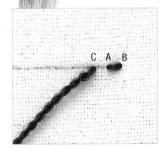

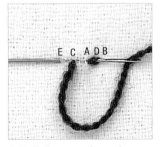

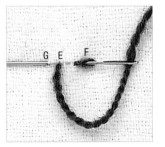

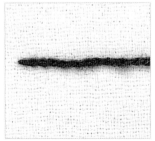

1 Bring the yarn to the front at A, a short distance from the right hand end. Take the needle from B to C and pull through.

2 Pull the yarn through. Take the needle from D to E, splitting the previous stitch. D is halfway between A and B.

3 Pull the yarn through. Take the needle from F to G, splitting the previous stitch.

4 Continue, keeping the stitches equal in length. For the last stitch, take the needle to the back through the previous stitch and end off.

STEM STITCH

Also known as:

- crewel stitch, South Kensington stitch

Stem stitch is very similar in appearance to outline stitch but the yarn is always kept below the needle, whereas in outline stitch, it is always kept above.

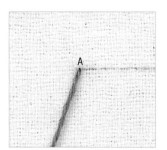

1 Bring the yarn to the front on the left hand side (A).

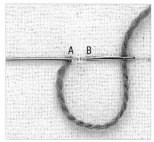

2 With the thread below, take the needle to the back at B and re-emerge at A.

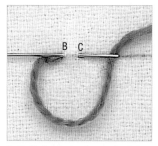

3 Pull the yarn through. Take the needle from C to B ensuring the yarn is below the needle.

4 Pull the yarn through. Continue working stitches in the same manner ensuring the needle always re-emerges at the beginning of the previous stitch.

5 Work the last stitch then take the needle to the back at the beginning of the previous stitch.

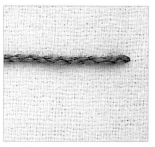

6 Pull the yarn through and end off on the back of the fabric.

STEM STITCH – WHIPPED

To create this stitch a foundation of stem stitch is first worked. The whipped stitches are worked over the foundation and do not go through the fabric. Use a tapestry needle for the whipping to help prevent splitting the foundation stitches.

1 Foundation. Work a line of stem stitch. **Whipping.** Bring a new thread to the front just above the first stem stitch.

2 Slide the needle from bottom to top under the space shared by the first and second stem stitches. Do not go through the fabric.

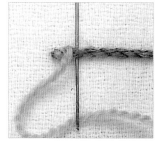

3 Pull the yarn through. Take the needle from bottom to top under the space shared by the second and third stem stitches.

4 Pull the yarn through. Continue to the end in the same manner. To end off, take the needle to the back behind the last stem stitch and secure.

STRAIGHT GOBELIN STITCH

Straight Gobelin stitch is worked on canvas from right to left and is made up of a series of vertical straight stitches worked over two or more canvas threads.

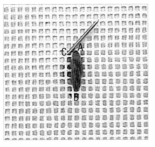

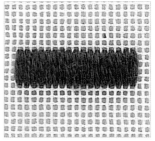

1 Secure the yarn on the back of the fabric. Bring the yarn to the front at A on the right hand side. Take the needle to the back at B.

2 Pull the yarn through. Re-emerge at C, in the next hole to the left of A.

3 Pull the yarn through. Take the needle to the back at D, one hole to the left of B.

4 Pull the yarn through. Continue working the desired number of stitches in the same manner. After the last stitch, secure the yarn on the back.

STRAIGHT STITCH

Also known as:

- stroke stitch

Straight stitch is the most basic embroidery stitch there is. It can be stitched in any direction and to any length, and it forms the basis of many other stitches.

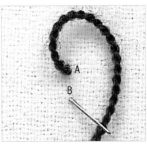

1 Bring the yarn to the front at the beginning of the stitch (A).

2 Take the needle to the back at the end of the stitch (B).

3 Pull the yarn through and end off on the back of the fabric.

4 Straight stitches worked at different angles.

Tapestry

Tapestry is a term which is often misused. It is sometimes used to refer to various forms of canvas work. In reality, tapestry is not a form of embroidery but a heavy ornamental fabric created by hand weaving. Tapestries, in the form of wall hangings and rugs, were used to provide comfort in the castles of medieval England and Europe. During the 16th and 17th centuries canvas work was used to recreate these tapestries and so the two techniques became confused.

TENT STITCH – CONTINENTAL

This canvas work stitch is a small diagonal stitch. Each one covers a single intersection of two canvas threads. It can be worked either horizontally or vertically.

 indicates top of fabric

1 **Working horizontally.** Bring the yarn to the front at A. Take the needle to the back at B, through the next hole above and to the right of A.

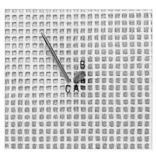

2 Pull the yarn through. Re-emerge at C, one hole to the left of A.

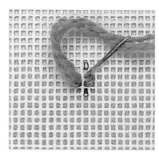

3 Take the yarn to the back at D, in the hole directly above A.

4 Pull the yarn through to complete the second stitch. Continue working stitches along the row in the same manner.

5 Turn the fabric upside down. Emerge at E.

6 Take the yarn to the back at F. Continue along the row in the same manner.

7 **Working vertically.** Bring the yarn to the front at A. Take the needle to the back at B.

8 Pull the yarn through. Re-emerge at C, directly below A.

9 Take the needle to the back at D, one hole to the right of A.

10 Pull the yarn through to complete the second stitch. Continue working stitches downwards in the same manner.

11 Work subsequent rows in the same manner, turning the fabric before beginning each one.

Pandora, Inspirations 5

TENT STITCH – HALF CROSS

On the front of the fabric, half cross stitch looks exactly the same as continental tent stitch. However, it is worked in a slightly different manner and as such, it uses less yarn and is less likely to distort the fabric.

↑ indicates top of fabric

1 Working horizontally.
Bring the yarn to the front at A. Take the needle to the back at B, one hole above and to the right of A.

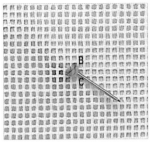

2 Pull the yarn through. Re-emerge at C, one hole directly below B.

3 Pull the yarn through. Take the needle to the back at D, one hole to the right of B.

4 Continue to the end of the row in the same manner.

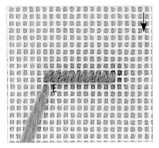

5 Turn the fabric upside down. Emerge at E.

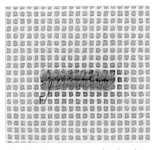

6 Take the yarn to the back at F. Continue along the row in the same manner.

7 Working vertically. Bring the yarn to the front at A. Take the needle to the back at B, through the next hole above and to the right of A.

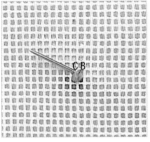

8 Pull the yarn through. Re-emerge at C, just to the left of B.

9 Take the needle to the back at D, one hole above and to the right of C.

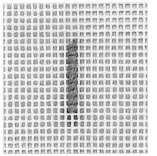

10 Pull the yarn through to complete the second stitch. Continue working stitches upwards in the same manner.

11 Work subsequent rows in the same manner, turning the fabric before beginning each one.

THREAD PAINTING

See: soft shading, page 48.

54

TRELLIS COUCHING

Trellis couching is a commonly used stitch in traditional crewel embroidery. It consists of a grid of long straight stitches couched in place with small crosses or straight stitches.

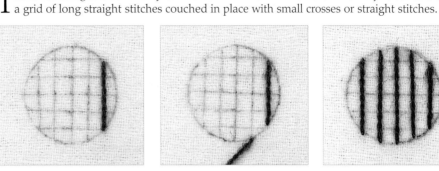

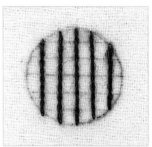

1 Foundation. Draw the outline of the shape and mark the grid lines. Bring the yarn to the front where one grid line meets the outline.

2 Take the yarn to the back of the fabric at the opposite end of the grid line.

3 Re-emerge on the next line across. Pull the yarn through.

4 Take the yarn to the back at the end of the grid line. Continue in the same manner until all the vertical grid lines are covered with stitches.

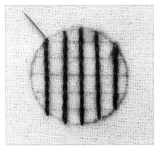

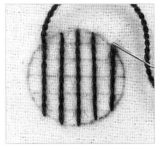

5 Bring the needle to the front on the left hand side of the outline where it meets one horizontal grid line.

6 Pull the yarn through. Take the needle over the previous straight stitches and to the back of the fabric at the opposite end of the grid line.

7 Continue working long straight stitches across the shape until all the grid lines are covered.

8 Couching. Using a different yarn, bring it to the front just below and to the left of one intersection of the foundation.

9 Take the needle to the back of the fabric just above and to the right of the intersection. Pull through. Re-emerge at the lower left of the next intersection.

10 Pull the yarn through. Continue working stitches to the end of the row. Bring the needle to the front just below and to the right of the last intersection.

11 Pull the yarn through. Take the yarn to the back diagonally opposite, forming a cross. Re-emerge just below and to the right of the next intersection.

12 Continue to the end of the row. Work all other rows in the same manner.

Also known as:

- plush stitch, Berlin plush stitch, Astrakhan stitch, rug stitch, raised stitch and tassel stitch

VELVET STITCH

Velvet stitch is a canvas work stitch. It was frequently used to create the plush three-dimensional areas of raised Berlin work.

1 **First row.** Bring the yarn to the front at A. Take the needle to the back of the fabric at B, two holes away diagonally to the right.

2 Pull the yarn through. Re-emerge at A, through exactly the same hole.

3 Pull the yarn through. Form a loop of the desired size and hold in place. Take the needle to the back at B.

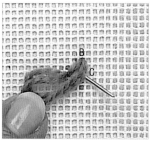

4 Pull the yarn through. Re-emerge at C, two holes below. Ensure the tip of the needle does not go through the loop.

5 Still holding the loop, pull the yarn through. Take the needle to the back at D, two holes to the left of B.

6 Pull the yarn through. Re-emerge at C.

7 To begin the second stitch, take the needle to the back of the fabric at E, two holes away diagonally to the right.

8 Pull the yarn through and complete the stitch following steps 2–6.

9 Continue working stitches in the same manner to the end of the row. To begin the next row, bring the yarn to the front at D.

10 Continue across the row as before. Work subsequent rows in the same manner.

11 Using small sharp scissors, cut through the loops as shown, one row at a time. Slightly tug the loops with the blade as you cut them.

12 Comb and trim the loops to the desired length.

WOOL ROSE

This quick and easy rose is created from a series of straight stitches. The size of the rose can be varied by changing the thickness of the yarn.

 indicates top of fabric

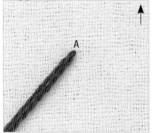

1 **Centre.** Bring the yarn to the front at A.

2 Take the needle to the back at B and re-emerge 1–2 fabric threads from A. The needle is slightly angled.

3 Pull the yarn through. Take a second stitch the same length, angling the needle as shown.

4 Pull the yarn through. Work three more stitches in the same manner. Take the needle to the back at C to complete the last stitch, forming a square.

5 Bring the needle to the front at D, through the same hole in the fabric as the previous stitch (A).

6 Pull the yarn through. Take the needle to the back at E using the same hole in the fabric as the stitch in the first layer.

7 Pull the yarn through. Bring the needle to the front just below D.

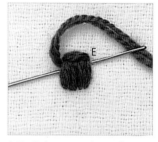

8 Pull the yarn through. Take the needle to the back just below E and bring it to the front on the opposite side directly below the emerging yarn.

9 Continue working stitches in the same manner until the first layer is completely covered. End off the yarn on the back.

10 **First petal.** Using a lighter shade, bring the yarn to the front at F.

11 Take the needle to the back at G.

12 Pull the yarn through. Re-emerge just to the right of F.

↑ indicates top of fabric

13 Take the needle to the back slightly higher and wider than G.

14 Pull the yarn through, positioning the stitch so it lies alongside the first stitch of the petal.

15 Bring the yarn to the front just to the right of where the previous stitch emerged.

16 Take the needle to the back slightly higher and wider than the previous stitch.

17 Pull the yarn through, positioning the stitch so it lies alongside the previous stitch.

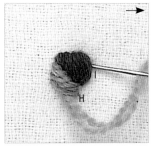

18 Second petal. Rotate the fabric a quarter turn. Bring the yarn to the front at H. Take the needle to the back at I.

19 Pull the yarn through.

20 Following steps 12–17, work two more stitches to complete the petal.

21 Third petal. Rotate the fabric a quarter turn. Bring the yarn to the front at J and take the needle to the back at K.

22 Pull the yarn through. Complete the petal following steps 12–17.

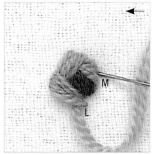

23 Fourth petal. Rotate the fabric a quarter turn. Bring the yarn to the front at L and take the needle to the back at M.

24 Pull the yarn through and complete the petal in the same manner as before.

WOVEN FILLING STITCH

Also known as:

- Queen Anne stitch

In this form of darning, yarn is woven across stitches to create the look of woven basketry. When weaving, use a tapestry needle or take the eye end of the needle through first.

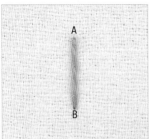

1 **Framework.** Bring the yarn to the front at A and take it to the back at B to form a long straight stitch.

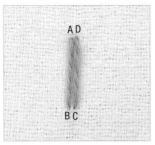

2 Re-emerge at C and work a second long straight stitch to D.

3 Continue working straight stitches in the same manner until the desired area is covered.

4 **Weaving.** Bring the yarn to the front at E, just to the right of the last vertical stitch and very close to the top of it.

5 Weave the needle over the last vertical stitch and under the stitch next to it.

6 Continue weaving over and under the stitches until reaching the left hand side. Pull the yarn through.

7 Take the needle to the back of the fabric at F, just to the left of the first vertical stitch and level with the line of weaving.

8 Pull the yarn through. Bring the needle to the front just below F.

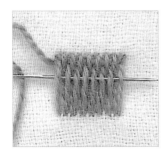

9 Pull the yarn through. Weave to the opposite side, ensuring you go over the vertical stitches you went under in the previous row and vice versa.

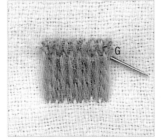

10 Pull the yarn through. Take the needle to the back at G. Pull the yarn through and re-emerge directly below G.

11 Weave across to the opposite side, following steps 5 and 6.

12 Continue working rows in the same manner until the vertical stitches are filled completely. Take the yarn to the back and end off.

Designs

BEAR

by Libby Vater

An adorable little sculpted bear cub, created with
Ghiordes knots, rests in a bed of field flowers.

This design uses

Back stitch, beading, bullion knot,
detached chain, fly stitch,
French knot, Ghiordes knot,
padded satin stitch, running stitch,
straight stitch, whipped back stitch

Order of work

Bear

Stitch the muzzle first, working upwards from the lower edge. Comb, then trim and shape the knots slightly. Stitch the head and then the ears, combing and trimming each area slightly when it is complete. Work the body and legs in the same manner. Trim and reshape all sections to sculpt the bear.

Using black thread, work long horizontal satin stitches over the Ghiordes knots to form the padding for the bear's nose. Embroider vertical satin stitches over the top. Stitch the mouth and attach the eyes.

White daisies

Embroider the stems and leaves first. Work the petals using the white mohair. Add the highlight to each petal with a straight stitch which lies alongside the mohair stitch. Secure 3–7 beads to the centre of each flower.

Pink daisies

Work the stems and leaves and then stitch the detached chain petals. Add a single French knot for the centre.

Forget-me-nots

Stitch five blue French knots for the petals and a yellow French knot for the centre of each flower. Work the stems in straight stitch.

Grasses and tiny flowers

Stitch the five tall clumps of grass first. Scatter straight stitches around the base of the bear for the remaining grass.

Dot French knots among the straight stitches for the tiny flowers.

Bee

Embroider the gold bullion knots first, using seven wraps in the end knots and nine wraps in the middle knot. Work a chocolate bullion knot of eight wraps in the spaces between the gold knots.

Add the eyes and then work a fly stitch around the bee's body. The anchoring stitch of the fly stitch becomes the bee's stinger.

Separate the strands of metallic thread and put them back together before working the wings. Stitch two Ghiordes knots on each side of the upper body for the wings. Do not cut the loops.

Finally, work the flight trail in running stitch with the metallic thread.

Types of wool

Wool is graded according to softness and smoothness. The finer the wool the softer and smoother it will be.

The finest wools come from Merino sheep. While merinos originated in Spain, today Australia leads the world in the breeding of these magnificent creatures and in the production of high quality merino wool.

Medium wools generally come from crossbred sheep. New Zealand and the United Kingdom produce much of the best wool of this type.

Coarse wool, which comes from Cheviot sheep, is mainly used for carpets, industrial felts and other furnishing fabrics.

BEAR

Requirements

Appletons 2 ply crewel wool
A = 142 vy lt dull rose pink
B = 181 ultra lt chocolate
C = 182 vy lt chocolate
D = 184 chocolate
E = 185 med chocolate
F = 187 vy dk chocolate
G = 741 ultra lt bright china blue

Anchor stranded cotton
H = 300 lt butter yellow
I = 311 straw
J = 381 vy dk chocolate
K = 403 black
L = 859 fern green
M = 860 dk fern green
N = 862 ultra dk fern green
O = 890 old gold

Rajmahal Art silk
P = 96 white
Q = 211 hyacinth

Mogear gossamer mohair
R = white
S = 17b lt pink
T = 18a dk pink
U = 39a lt green

DMC stranded metallic thread
V = 5282 gold

Mill Hill glass seed beads
W = 00275 coral

Black shank buttons 7mm (⁵⁄₁₆″) wide
for the bear's eyes.

Embroidery key

All embroidery is worked with two strands unless otherwise specified.

Bear

Head = C, E and F (Ghiordes knot)
Muzzle = C (Ghiordes knot)
Muzzle outline = F (Ghiordes knot)
Inner ears = A and B (Ghiordes knot)
Outer ears = D and F (Ghiordes knot)
Body = B, C, D, E and F (Ghiordes knot)
Legs = C, D, E and F (Ghiordes knot)
Paw pads = A (Ghiordes knot)
Nose = K (padded satin stitch)
Mouth = K (back stitch)
Eyes = buttons

White daisies

Petals = R (1 strand, straight stitch)
Petal highlights = P (1 strand, straight stitch)
Centre = W (beading)
Stems = L (back stitch), M (1 strand, whipping)
Leaves = L (detached chain)

Pink daisies

Petals = T (1 strand, detached chain)
Centre = I (6 strands, French knot, 1 wrap)
Stems = N (1 strand, whipped back stitch)
Leaves = N (1 strand, fly stitch)

Forget-me-nots

Petals = G (French knot, 1 wrap)
Centre = H (6 strands, French knot, 1 wrap)
Stems = U (1 strand, straight stitch)

Grasses and tiny flowers

Tall clumps = N (straight stitch)
Scattered grass = L and M (straight stitch), U (1 strand, straight stitch)
Tiny flowers = N (French knot, 2 wraps), Q (3 strands, French knot, 2 wraps), S and T (1 strand, French knot, 2 wraps)

Bee

Body = J and O (3 strands, bullion knot, 7–9 wraps)
Eyes = J (3 strands, French knot, 2 wraps)
Body outline and stinger = J (1 strand, fly stitch)
Wings = V (Ghiordes knot)
Flight trail = V (1 strand, running stitch)

Whipping stitch

Whipping is a combination stitch where a second thread is worked over a foundation line of another stitch. It can be worked over a multitude of stitches, as well as over a couched yarn.

CHICKEN
by Susan O'Connor

This cute, fluffy chicken is surrounded with kernels of golden corn.

This design uses

Back stitch, French knot,
long and short stitch,
padded satin stitch, satin stitch,
seed stitch, soft shading,
split stitch, straight stitch

Order of work

Chicken

Using D, embroider the head and tail
in long and short stitch. Work the area
surrounding the eye and fill in the wing.
Stitching from the head, fill in
approximately half the body with B.
Change to two strands of D and fill the
remainder of the body.

Stitch the outlines, shadows and then
the highlights. Fill each half of the beak
and work back stitches along the
middle. Work the eye in satin stitch
and add a seed stitch over the top.

Work long straight stitches along the
legs and claws for padding. Cover these
stitches withsatin stitch.

Corn

Work three straight stitches for each
kernel of corn.

Requirements

Appletons 2 ply crewel wool
A = 471 ultra lt autumn yellow
B = 473 lt autumn yellow
C = 475 med autumn yellow
D = 694 med honeysuckle yellow
DMC broder médicis 1 ply wool
E = 8328 vy lt yellow
DMC tapestry wool
F = 7472 lt autumn yellow
G = 7767 med autumn yellow
Madeira stranded silk
H = 2400 black
I = 2207 vy lt old gold

Embroidery key

*All embroidery is worked with one strand unless
otherwise specified.*

Chicken

Head and body = D (long and short stitch), B and D
(2 strands, long and short stitch)

Outlines = C (split stitch)

Wings = A (long and short stitch)

Tail = D (long and short stitch)

Shadows = C (straight stitch)

Highlights = E (straight stitch)

Beak = I (4 strands, satin stitch, back stitch)

Eye = H (4 strands, satin stitch), I (4 strands,
seed stitch)

Eye surround = A (long and short stitch)

Legs = G (straight stitch), C (2 strands, padded
satin stitch)

Corn

Kernels = F (straight stitch)

BABY BIRDS
by Margo Fanning

Three plump chicks perch precariously among the apple blossoms.

This design uses

Back stitch, blanket stitch,
bullion knot, colonial knot,
couching, detached chain, fly stitch,
long and short stitch, pistil stitch,
satin stitch, seed stitch, soft shading,
stem stitch, straight stitch

Order of work

Branch

Lay down six strands of yarn for the main branch and couch in place. Use four strands of yarn for the secondary branches and two strands for the twigs. Vary the spacing between the couching stitches.

Birds

Using O, completely cover each bird with long and short stitches. Ensure the stitches lie in the same direction as feathers on a bird. Add long and short stitches in P to the body of the left bird only.

Work long straight stitches over the breasts, blending the shades of grey. Add a few straight stitches in the darkest grey to the middle of the head.

Embroider the eyes with black satin stitches and add a tiny seed stitch over the top. Surround each eye with a semicircle of back stitches.

Stitch two bullion knots, one above the other, for the beak of the left bird. Work two bullion knots for the upper beaks of the remaining birds. Couch the knots in place. Use straight stitches for the lower beak of the middle bird and stem stitches for the lower beak of the right bird.

Flowers

Embroider the petals in long and short stitch, grading from the lighter colour at the outer edge to the darker in the centre. For the curling petals, work the outer half in blanket stitch with the 'purls' towards the centre.

Work a cluster of colonial knots in the centre of each flower except for the three-petalled flower on the right. Fill the centre of this flower with a mix of colonial knots and pistil stitches.

Foliage

Following the photograph, work the leaves in fly stitch and satin stitch. Add a short straight stitch to the base of each satin stitched leaf for stems.

Requirements

Appletons 2 ply crewel wool
A = 242 lt olive green
B = 251 vy lt grass green
C = 311 ultra lt brown olive
D = 343 lt mid olive green
E = 752 vy lt rose pink
F = 991 white
G = 993 black
Kacoonda hand dyed medium embroidery wool
H = 108 variegated rose
DMC broder médicis 1 ply wool
I = 8422 dk sage
J = 8506 dk steel grey
K = 8508 lt steel grey
L = 8509 vy lt steel grey
DMC tapestry wool
M = 7061 med beige
N = 7275 dk storm grey
Marta's Yarns 2 ply wool
O = 1563 lt blue-grey
P = 1565 dk blue-grey

Embroidery key

All embroidery is worked with one strand unless otherwise specified.

Branches and twigs = N (2–6 strands, laid yarn), M (couching)

Birds

Head and body = O and P (long and short stitch)

Breast = J, K and L (straight stitch)

Above beak = J (straight stitch)

Eyes = G (satin stitch), L (back stitch, seed stitch)

Beak = C (2 strands, straight stitch, stem stitch, bullion knot, 14–16 wraps)

Flowers

Petals = F (long and short stitch), E and H (blanket stitch, long and short stitch)

Centre = C (colonial knot, pistil stitch)

Bud = E and H (straight stitch)

Bud calyx = I (2 strands, detached chain), D (straight stitch)

Foliage

Leaves = A and I (satin stitch, fly stitch, straight stitch), D (satin stitch, straight stitch), B (satin stitch)

Vein on left leaf = B (2 strands, back stitch)

Pistil stitch

Pistil stitch is a French knot on a stem (see page 33 for French knots). Varying the length of the stem and the number of wraps in the knot will give different effects. Pistil stitches are often used for flower stamens and petals.

For a curved effect, loosen the tension as you place the stitch for the stem.

BLUE WREN
by Margo Fanning

A cheeky blue wren eyes its next meal while a tiny pygmy possum crouches among the thryptomene flowers. The technique of soft shading is used to create the lifelike appearance of these dear little creatures.

This design uses
Bullion knot, cross stitch, detached chain, long and short stitch, soft shading, stem stitch, straight stitch, whipped stem stitch

Order of work

Thryptomene

Work the stems first and then the leaves. Stitch five petals, each with two straight stitches, for the flowers.

Blue wren

Begin stitching at the head and work towards the back and legs. Work the stitches in the same direction as the feathers would lie.

Using the two lighter shades of blue, cover the tail with straight stitches. Embroider a second layer of straight stitches over the first with the two grey yarns.

Work the eye, stitching the white section over the grey. Finally, stitch the legs and claws.

Pygmy possum

Work the head and body in long and short stitch, leaving spaces for the eyes. Embroider six bullion knots for the claws, taking the knots over the thryptomene stem. Stitch the eyes in the same manner as the blue wren's, then outline the ears and add the whiskers with straight stitches in the darkest grey yarn.

Fly

Work a cross stitch for the head and four detached chains for the wings.

Requirements

Appletons 2 ply crewel wool
A = 144 dull rose pink
B = 293 lt Jacobean green
C = 346 dk mid olive green
D = 742 vy lt bright china blue
E = 752 vy lt rose pink
F = 822 lt royal blue
G = 974 elephant grey
H = 975 dk elephant grey
I = 976 vy dk elephant grey
J = 986 brown putty groundings
K = 991B bright white
L = 993 black

DMC broder médicis 1 ply wool
M = 8200 French navy
N = 8502 vy lt fawn

Embroidery key

All embroidery is worked with one strand unless otherwise specified.

Thryptomene

Flowers = A and E (straight stitch)

Stems = H (whipped stem stitch)

Leaves = B and C (straight stitch)

Blue wren

Head and breast = D, F and L (long and short stitch), M (2 strands, long and short stitch)

Tail = D, F, G and I (straight stitch)

Back and wing = G and I (long and short stitch)

Stomach = K (long and short stitch), N (2 strands, long and short stitch)

Beak = L and M (long and short stitch)

Eye = I and K (straight stitch)

Legs = G (whipped stem stitch)

Claws = G (straight stitch)

Pygmy possum

Head and body = J (long and short stitch)

Ear outlines = I (straight stitch, stem stitch)

Eyes = K and M (straight stitch)

Eye surrounds = N (straight stitch)

Claws = J (bullion knot, 5 wraps)

Tail = J (whipped stem stitch)

Whiskers = I (straight stitch)

Fly

Head = H (cross stitch)

Wings = H (detached chain)

BUTTERFLIES
by Susan O'Connor

The colour and movement of these exotic butterflies are captured with woollen yarns and simple stitches.

This design uses

Back stitch, fly stitch, French knot, long and short stitch, satin stitch, split stitch, straight stitch

Order of work

Each butterfly is stitched in a similar manner. Embroider the wings first and then the body. Add the outlines. Stitch any wing markings over the previous stitching. Finally work the antennae and eyes.

Butterfly 1

Requirements

Appletons 2 ply crewel wool
A = 224 bright terracotta
B = 297 dk Jacobean green
C = 316 dk brown olive
D = 333 lt drab green
E = 335 med drab green
F = 428 dk leaf green
G = 448 dk orange red
H = 471 ultra lt autumn yellow
I = 473 lt autumn yellow
J = 475 med autumn yellow
K = 503 med scarlet
L = 504 dk scarlet
M = 587 brown groundings
N = 695 honeysuckle yellow
O = 713 lt wine red
P = 714 med wine red
Q = 745 bright china blue
R = 751 ultra lt rose pink
S = 754 med rose pink
T = 873 vy lt mint green
U = 874 lt mint green
Paterna Persian yarn
V = D117 dk basil
W = 341 med periwinkle
X = 564 vy lt glacier
Y = 751 dk old gold

Embroidery key

All embroidery is worked with one strand unless otherwise specified.

Butterfly 1

Upper wings = D and X (long and short stitch)

Spots on upper wings = A and H (satin stitch, straight stitch)

Lower wings = A and X (long and short stitch, satin stitch)

Thorax and abdomen = C (satin stitch)

Wing outlines = B (back stitch)

Thorax outline = B (back stitch)

Abdomen outline = M (back stitch)

Antennae = M (back stitch, straight stitch)

Eyes = B (straight stitch)

Butterfly 2

Upper wings = G (long and short stitch)

Spots on upper wings = F (straight stitch, French knot, 2 wraps)

Lower wings = E (satin stitch)

Body = J (satin stitch)

Wing outlines and markings = B (back stitch)

Body outline = B (back stitch)

Antennae = M (back stitch, French knot, 1 wrap)

Eyes = B (straight stitch)

Butterfly 3

Left upper wing = P (long and short stitch)

Spots on left upper wing = I (satin stitch, straight stitch)

Right upper wing = O (satin stitch)

Lower wing = K and L (long and short stitch)

Body = C (satin stitch)

Wing outlines = B (back stitch)

Body outline = M (back stitch)

Antennae = M (back stitch, French knot, 1 wrap)

Eyes = B (straight stitch)

Butterfly 3

Butterfly 2

Butterfly 4

Butterfly 6

Butterfly 4

Inner left wing = S (long and short stitch),
D (satin stitch)

Outer left wing = Y (satin stitch)

Spots on left wing = W (satin stitch, straight stitch)

Inner right wing = R (long and short stitch)

Outer right wing = N (satin stitch)

Thorax = C (French knot, 1 wrap)

Abdomen = C (satin stitch)

Wing outlines = B (back stitch), A (split stitch)

Wing markings = B (back stitch)

Abdomen outline = M (back stitch)

Antennae = M (back stitch,
French knot, 1 wrap)

Eyes = B (straight stitch)

Butterfly 5

Upper wings = U (long and short stitch)

Wing markings = P (French knot, 2 wraps),
B (fly stitch)

Lower wings = V (satin stitch)

Body = J (satin stitch)

Wing outlines = B (back stitch)

Body outline = M (back stitch)

Antennae = M (back stitch,
French knot, 1 wrap)

Eyes = B (straight stitch)

Butterfly 6

Upper wings = T (long and short stitch),
W (satin stitch)

Spots = S (satin stitch, straight stitch)

Lower wings = I (long and short stitch)

Thorax = Y (French knot, 1 wrap)

Abdomen = Y (satin stitch)

Wing outlines = B (back stitch)

Antennae = M (back stitch,
straight stitch)

Eyes = B (straight stitch)

Butterfly 7

Upper wings = Q (long and short stitch)

Spots on wings = J (satin stitch, straight stitch)

Lower wings = F (long and short stitch)

Body = C (satin stitch)

Wing outlines = B (back stitch)

Body outline = M (back stitch)

Antennae = M (back stitch, straight stitch)

Eyes = B (straight stitch)

Butterfly 7

Butterfly 5

Butterfly Dreaming, Inspirations 5

KOALA
by Jenny McWhinney

Nestled high in the fork of a flowering eucalypt, this fluffy eared koala is realistically rendered in very fine wool.

This design uses

Back stitch, fly stitch,
French knot, Ghiordes knot,
long and short stitch, satin stitch,
soft shading, stem stitch, straight stitch

Order of work

Koala

Embroider the head from the outer edge towards the nose, leaving spaces for the eyes, nose and mouth. Add the facial features and then work the highlights around them.

Stitch the body next and then the legs. Scatter ecru straight stitches over the upper part of the body to create flecks of white fur.

Work the paw pad on the left foot with black long and short stitches and partially outline it with pink stem stitches.

Stitch the ears with rows of closely packed Ghiordes knots, leaving the loops approximately 1cm (⅜") long. Comb and trim the loops until the yarn is fluffy and approximately 6mm (¼") long.

Embroider the claws after the gum tree is worked.

Gum tree

Using the photograph as a guide to colour placement, work the trunk and main branches in long and short stitch. Change the direction of stitching for the smaller branches. Embroider the twigs and then the leaves. Stitch the tiny gum blossoms with French knots and add their stems with fly stitches.

Requirements

DMC broder médicis 1 ply wool
A = ecru
B = noir
C = 8135 dk coral
D = 8211 pearl grey
E = 8224 lt shell pink
F = 8302 med tan
G = 8313 bright mustard
H = 8322 lt tan
I = 8381 vy lt warm grey
J = 8503 grey-fawn
K = 8504 lt fawn
L = 8506 dk steel grey
M = 8507 med steel grey
N = 8508 lt steel grey
O = 8515 vy lt camel
P = 8748 pale yellow
Q = 8839 dk mocha
R = 8841 lt mocha
S = 8877 pewter

Torokina Yarns hand dyed embroidery wool
T = 253 eucalyptus

DMC stranded cotton
U = 780 ultra dk topaz
V = 830 dk golden olive

Embroidery key

All embroidery is worked with one strand unless otherwise specified.

Koala

Head = D and S (long and short stitch, straight stitch), A and J (straight stitch)

Body = D, I, K, O and R (long and short stitch, straight stitch), A (straight stitch)

Legs = D, I, L, M, N and S (long and short stitch)

Claws = B, E and L (long and short stitch, straight stitch)

Base of left foot = B (long and short stitch), E (stem stitch)

Ears = A, D, M, N and S (Ghiordes knot, 2 strands,)

Eyes = Q (satin stitch), B (back stitch, straight stitch), A (straight stitch)

Nose = L (satin stitch), B (back stitch, straight stitch)

Nostrils = E (straight stitch)

Mouth = E (long and short stitch, back stitch), Q (back stitch)

Highlights around eyes = A (straight stitch)

Highlights around nose = O (straight stitch)

Highlights below mouth = A (long and short stitch)

Gum tree

Trunk and branches = F, G, H, J, P and Q (long and short stitch)

Twigs = F, H, J and Q (back stitch, straight stitch)

Leaves = T (long and short stitch)

Blossoms = C (French knot, 1–3 wraps)

Blossom stems = U and V (fly stitch)

RABBIT
by Jenny McWhinney

Worked in soft shades of brown, this realistic little rabbit bounces
over a bed of tiny spring flowers.

This design uses
Back stitch, bullion knot, couching, detached chain, fly stitch, French knot,
long and short stitch, satin stitch, soft shading, split stitch, straight stitch

Order of work

Rabbit

Using the lightest brown yarn, outline the rabbit in split stitch. Beginning at the white eye area and working outwards, fill the head and ears with long and short stitch. Allow the stitches of one colour to blend with the stitches of a new colour. Place the stitches in the same directions as the lines on the pattern (see page 116). Ensure the split stitch outlines are completely covered. When working the inner ear, shade from the darker pink at the base to the lighter pink at the tip. Work the body, legs and tail in the same manner. Scatter straight stitches over the tail using the lightest brown yarn.

Embroider the nose and paw pads in satin stitch. Partially outline the legs, back and face using back stitch and split stitch.

Flowers

Stitch the roses first, using three bullion knots for the centre of the larger roses and two bullion knots for the centre of the smaller roses. Couch the bullion knots in place.

Work the leaves followed by the blue daisies. Stitch clusters of mauve and yellow French knots among the larger flowers and leaves for alyssum and primroses.

Requirements

Appletons 2 ply crewel wool
A = 341 ultra lt mid olive green
B = 343 lt mid olive green
C = 603 med mauve
D = 752 vy lt rose pink
E = 753 lt rose pink
F = 761 ultra lt biscuit brown
G = 764 biscuit brown
H = 765 med biscuit brown
I = 882 cream
J = 893 med hyacinth
K = 911B bright white
L = 996 lemon
Madeira stranded silk
M = 2400 black

Embroidery key

All embroidery is worked with one strand unless otherwise specified.
Rabbit
Eye = M (2 strands, satin stitch, back stitch)
Fur around eye = I (long and short stitch)
Cheeks = I (long and short stitch)
Nose = E (satin stitch)
Inner ears = D and E (long and short stitch)
Outer ears = F, G and H (long and short stitch)
Paw pads = E (straight stitch)
Head and body = F, G, H and I (long and short stitch)
Legs = F, G, H and I (long and short stitch)

Tail = K (long and short stitch), F (straight stitch)
Teeth = K (satin stitch)
Partial outlines = G and H (split stitch, back stitch)
Roses
Centre = E (2–3 bullion knots, 4–5 wraps, couching)
Inner petals = E (3–5 bullion knots, 6–10 wraps, couching)
Outer petals = D (3–4 bullion knots, 6–10 wraps, couching)
Leaves
Light green leaves = A (fly stitch)
Dark green leaves = B (fly stitch)
Blue daisies
Petals = J (detached chain)
Centre = J (French knot, 1–2 wraps) or none
Mauve alyssum = C (French knot, 1–2 wraps)
Yellow primroses = L (French knot, 1–2 wraps)

BASKET OF ROSES
by Kris Richards

These glorious pink roses and blue forget-me-nots could have been freshly picked from the garden and artfully arranged in the rustic woven basket.

Order of work

Basket

Using the brown yarn, work the basket with woven filling stitch. Add two rows of stem stitch for the base.

Flowers

Work the six roses following the embroidery key for colour and yarn changes.

Using the pale blue yarn, work granitos for each forget-me-not petal.

Following the embroidery key and photograph for colour change and placement, fill in the spaces around the roses and forget-me-nots with French knot buds.

Work the leaves using the three shades of green. Place them around the outer edge of the flowers and over the top edge of the basket.

Requirements

DMC tapestry wool
A = 7226 dk dusky pink
B = 7335 med sage green
DMC broder médicis 1 ply wool
C = 8402 avocado
Paterna Persian yarn
D = 344 ultra lt periwinkle
E = 534 lt blue spruce
F = 642 khaki green
G = 651 olive green
H = 804 lt marigold
Appletons 2 ply crewel wool
I = 754 med lt rose pink
J = 762 vy lt biscuit brown
**Gumnut Yarns 'Blossoms'
2 ply crewel wool**
K = 013 pale baby pink
L = 850 vy pale baby pink

Embroidery key

All embroidery is worked with one strand unless otherwise specified.

Basket = J (2 strands, woven filling stitch, stem stitch)

Large roses

Centre = I (bullion knot, 6 wraps)
Inner petals = K (3 bullion knots, 10 wraps)
Outer petals = L (3 or 5 bullion knots, 10 wraps)

Medium roses

Centre = K (2 bullion knots, 6–8 wraps)
Petals = L (5 bullion knots, 12 wraps)

Small roses

Centre = K (2 bullion knots, 6–8 wraps)
Petals = L (3 bullion knots, 10–12 wraps)

Forget-me-nots = D (granitos)

French knot buds = A, B, E and H (French knot, 1 wrap)

Leaves = C, F and G (detached chain)

ROSEBUD BOUQUET
by Annie Humphris

A bouquet of three large pink buds, encircled with forget-me-nots, is tied with an elaborate pale blue bow.

This design uses

Back stitch, detached chain, fly stitch, French knot, granitos, running stitch, straight stitch

Golden Embers, Inspirations 13

Order of work

Embroider the pink buds first, working a granitos of 6–7 straight stitches for the centre petal and another two of 3–4 straight stitches for the outer petals. Angle the outer petals across the centre petal. Stitch the calyx for each bud next, using straight stitch and detached chain. Stitch the stems and then add the highlights to the petals, calyxes and stems. Work a fly stitch to the tip of each bud for the stamens.

Embroider the four petals of the forget-me-nots with two straight stitches and then the French knot centres. Stitch the fronds and, finally, the bow.

Requirements

Appletons 2 ply crewel wool
A = 141 ultra lt dull rose pink
B = 142 vy lt dull rose pink
C = 181 ultra lt chocolate
D = 291 ultra lt Jacobean green
E = 461 vy lt cornflower blue
Anchor Marlitt stranded rayon
F = 868 old gold
G = 872 lt putty groundings
Anchor stranded cotton
H = 858 lt fern green

Embroidery key

All embroidery is worked with one strand unless otherwise specified.

Pink buds

Inner petal = B (granitos)

Left outer petal = C (granitos)

Right outer petal = A (granitos)

Stamens = G (fly stitch)

Calyx = D (detached chain, straight stitch)

Stem = D (back stitch)

Highlights = G (straight stitch)

Forget-me-nots

Petals = E (straight stitch)

Centre = F (2 strands, French knot, 1 wrap)

Fronds

Stem = H (running stitch)

Leaves = H (detached chain)

Bow

Loops = E blended with G (1 strand of each, detached chain)

Ties = E blended with G (1 strand of each, straight stitch)

Knot = E blended with G (1 strand of each, French knot, 1 wrap)

HEART OF BLOSSOMS
by Carolyn Pearce

In this romantic design, two delicate sprays of softly shaded blossoms and buds gently entwine to form a heart.

This design uses

Colonial knot, couching, detached chain, feather stitch, fly stitch, French knot, granitos, smocker's knot, straight stitch, whipping

Order of work

Embroider the five pink blossoms following the step-by-step instructions on page 78 and then the three blue blossoms in a similar manner. Add feather stitch tendrils around the blue blossoms.

Follow the instructions on page 79 to work the large pink buds. Stitch a granitos of five straight stitches for the petal of each small pink bud. Add a tiny granitos of five straight stitches just below the petal and then work straight stitches over the petal for the remainder of the calyx. Add the stamens in the same manner as those on the large buds.

Stitch a granitos of 3–4 straight stitches for each blue bud. Add dark blue stitches over the tip and then work the calyx and stems.

Embroider the forget-me-nots next. Work all remaining stems and the large fly stitch leaves. Stitch the silk ribbon buds and leaves last.

Requirements

Appletons 2 ply crewel wool

A = 292 vy lt Jacobean green
B = 461 vy lt cornflower blue
C = 472 vy lt autumn yellow
D = 602 lt mauve
E = 641 vy lt peacock
F = 642 lt peacock
G = 742 vy lt bright china blue
H = 743 lt bright china blue
I = 751 ultra lt rose pink
J = 753 lt rose pink
K = 754 med rose pink
L = 851 custard yellow
M = 877 pastel pink

DMC broder médicis 1 ply wool

N = 8405 vy lt sage green
O = 8406 med pistachio

Madeira stranded silk

P = 2400 black
Q = 1703 blue-green
R = 2114 hazelnut brown

Kanagawa 1000 denier silk thread

S = 170 dusky pink

Rajmahal Art silk

T = 311 Fresco oil
U = 421 green earth

DMC stranded cotton

V = 370 med verdigris

Kacoonda pure silk thread

W = 8C med variegated green-blue

YLI pure silk ribbon 4mm (³⁄₁₆″) wide

X = 1m (39½″) no. 163 rose
Y = 1m (39½″) no. 32 med pistachio

Embroidery key

All embroidery is worked with one strand unless otherwise specified.

Dark pink blossoms

Petals = J (2 strands, granitos)
Between petals = A (straight stitch)
Petal tips = D (straight stitch, fly stitch)
Highlights = S (straight stitch)
Centre = L and R blended together (1 strand of each, French knot, 3 wraps), C and P blended together (1 strand of each, French knot, 3 wraps)

Light pink blossoms

Petals = I (2 strands, granitos)
Between petals = A (straight stitch)
Petal tips = J (straight stitch, fly stitch)
Petal markings = S (straight stitch)
Centre = L and R blended together (1 strand of each, French knot, 3 wraps), C and P blended together (1 strand of each, French knot, 3 wraps)

Variegated blossoms

Petals = I and M blended together (1 strand of each, granitos)
Between petals = A (straight stitch)
Petal tips = J (straight stitch, fly stitch)
Highlights = S (straight stitch)
Centre = L and R blended together (1 strand of each, French knot, 3 wraps), C and P blended together (1 strand of each, French knot, 3 wraps)

Blue blossoms

Petals = B (2 strands, granitos)
Between petals = G (straight stitch)
Tip = G (straight stitch, fly stitch)
Centre = A and J blended together (1 strand of each, French knot, 3 wraps)
Leaves = N (feather stitch)

Large pink buds

Inner petal = K (2 strands, granitos)
Outer petals = I and J (2 strands, granitos)
Calyx = A, Q and U (straight stitch, granitos)
Stamens = U (fly stitch)
Stem = A (couching), U (whipping)

Small dark pink bud

Petal = J (2 strands, granitos)
Calyx = A and U (granitos, straight stitch)
Stamens = U (fly stitch)
Stem = A (couching), U (whipping)

Small light pink bud

Petal = I (2 strands, granitos)
Calyx = A and T (granitos, straight stitch)
Stamens = T (fly stitch)
Stem = A (couching), T (whipping)

Small variegated pink bud

Petal = I and M blended together (1 strand of each, granitos)
Calyx = A and T (granitos, straight stitch)
Stamens = T (fly stitch)
Stem = A (couching), T (whipping)

Blue buds

Bud = B (2 strands, granitos)
Tip = G (straight stitch, fly stitch)
Calyx = N (smocker's knot)
Stem = N (couching)

Forget-me-nots

Petals = H (2 strands, colonial knot)
Centre = 2 strands of L and 1 strand of R blended together (colonial knot)
Leaf = N (detached chain)
Leaf tip = U (straight stitch)

Large leaves

Leaf 1 = A (fly stitch, smocker's knot), V (straight stitch)
Leaf 2 = A (fly stitch, smocker's knot), T (straight stitch)
Leaf 3 = E (fly stitch, smocker's knot), W (straight stitch)
Leaf 4 = F (fly stitch, smocker's knot), U (straight stitch)

Silk ribbon buds

Petals = X (straight stitch)
Calyx = O (smocker's knot)
Leaf = Y (detached chain)
Leaf tip = Q (straight stitch)
Base of leaf = O (smocker's knot)
Stems = O (couching), Q (whipping)

Smocker's knot

A smocker's knot is firmer than a French knot (see page 33). In smocking and other embroidery it is often used as a secure technique for finishing off on the back of the work. It can also be used as a decorative stitch.

STEP-BY-STEP BLOSSOM

A combination of stitches is used to create this beautiful blossom. Each petal is a granitos. Fly and straight stitches add detail to the petals and French knots fill the centre.

1 **Petals.** Draw a circle for the blossom centre. Mark five dots for the tips of the petals. Bring the yarn to the front at A. Take the needle from B to A.

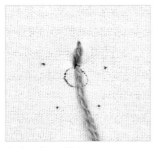

2 Gently pull the yarn through to form a straight stitch.

3 With the yarn to the left of the needle, take a second stitch from B to A.

4 Pull through. Leaving the yarn loose, place the needle under the stitch. This helps to create even, plump petals.

5 Keeping the needle under the stitch, pull the yarn until the second stitch lies to the left and snug against the first stitch.

6 Remove the needle from under the stitches. With the yarn to the right, take a third stitch from B to A.

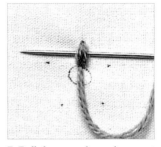

7 Pull the yarn through, placing the needle under the stitches as before. Pull until the stitch lies to the right of and snug against the first stitch.

8 Work 3–5 more stitches in the same manner. Lay the last three stitches over the top of the petal.

9 Work four more petals following steps 1–8. The petals just touch each other on the centre circle.

10 **Straight stitches between petals.** Change yarn. Work a straight stitch between each petal, stitching from the centre to where the petals separate.

11 **Petal tips.** Change yarn. Work a straight stitch from the centre of the petal to the tip and then a fly stitch around the tip of each petal.

12 Work three straight stitches over the petals for highlights. Fill the centre with closely packed French knots.

STEP-BY-STEP BUD

A combination of couching, whipping, straight stitch, fly stitch and granitos is used to create this lovely bud.

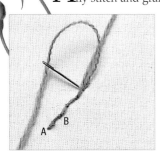

1 Stem. Bring the yarn to front at A and place it along the marked line. Bring a second yarn to the front at B and couch the laid yarn in place. Leave the yarns dangling.

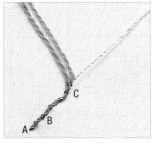

2 Bring the whipping thread to the front near A. Whip the couched yarn to C. Leave the thread and yarns dangling.

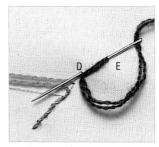

3 Inner petal. Using the darkest yarn, bring it to the front at D. Work a straight stitch from E to D. Take the needle from E to D again.

4 Work 4–5 more straight stitches in the same manner as the blossom petals to form a granitos.

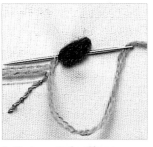

5 Outer petals. Change yarn. Bring it to the front, just left of the base of the first petal. Take needle to the back on right hand side approx. two thirds up the side.

6 Pull the yarn through. Work 2–3 more stitches using the same holes in the fabric.

7 Change yarn. Bring it to the front just to the right of D. Work this petal in the same manner as the previous petal but to the left.

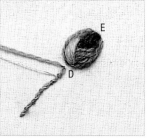

8 Calyx. Re-thread needle with the laid yarn. Take it to the back at D and re-emerge at E. Work two straight stitches on each side of the bud.

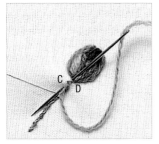

9 Work three straight stitches over the top of the bud. Re-thread the couching yarn. Take the needle to the back at D and re-emerge at C.

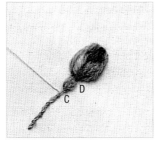

10 Work a granitos of 4–5 stitches between D and C. End off the yarn.

11 Highlights. Using the whipping thread, work three straight stitches over the granitos for the calyx and 8–10 straight stitches over the petals.

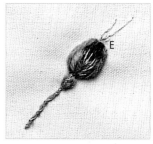

12 Stamens. Bring the same thread to the front near E. Turn the fabric upside down. Work two fly stitches, one long and one short, at the tip of the bud.

BOUQUET OF DAISIES
by Kris Richards

The rich hues of the plum and purple French knot buds are the perfect foil for the delicate daisies in soft shades of cream, pink and lavender.

This design uses
Detached chain, French knot, straight stitch

Order of work

Embroider the seven daisies in straight stitch first. Work a blue French knot in the centre of the top daisy and a yellow French knot in the centre of the two cream daisies.

Stitch the petals of the periwinkle blue daisies with detached chains. Add a large French knot to the centre of each one.

Randomly scatter French knot buds among the daisies. Work pairs of detached chain leaves around the outer edge of the bouquet.

Finally stitch five straight stitches for the stems of the bouquet.

Requirements
DMC tapestry wool
A = 7266 dk antique rose pink
Paterna Persian yarn
B = D117 dk basil
C = 262 cream
D = 312 med grape
E = 326 vy lt plum
F = 344 ultra lt periwinkle
G = 534 lt blue spruce
H = 652 bright olive green
I = 924 pale wood rose
Appletons 2 ply crewel wool
J = 851 custard yellow

Embroidery key

All embroidery is worked with one strand.

Purple daisy

Petals = D (straight stitch)

Centre = B (French knot, 1 wrap)

Pink daisy

Petals = I (straight stitch)

Pale pink daisies

Petals = E (straight stitch)

Cream daisies

Petals = C (straight stitch)

Centre = J (French knot, 1–2 wraps)

Blue daisies

Petals = F (detached chain)

Centre = F (French knot, 1 wrap)

Leaves = G and H (detached chain)

French knot buds = A and B
(French knot, 1 wrap)

Stems = G (straight stitch)

CREWEL SAMPLER
by Jean Harry

Traditional Jacobean stitches and motifs are used in this beautiful example of crewel embroidery.

This design uses
Blanket stitch, coral stitch, couching, cretan stitch, French knot, laid work, Palestrina stitch, satin stitch, seed stitch, split stitch, stem stitch, trellis couching

CREWEL SAMPLER

Order of work

Middle leaf

Beginning at the tip, work the centre in cretan stitch. Embroider two rows of stem stitch for the upper outline, using the lighter shades of green and blue. Change to the darker shades for the lower outline.

Right leaf

Work four rows of coral stitch for the lower half of the leaf. Shade from the lightest green on the top to the darkest green at the lower edge.

The upper half of the leaf is worked in stem stitch using three shades in each row. For both the blue and green rows, begin with the lightest shade on the left hand side and grade to the darkest on the right hand side.

Left leaf

Work five rows of coral stitch for the upper half. Stitch the lower half in a similar manner to the upper half of the right leaf.

Stems and tendril

Begin each row at the base and work towards the top. Using G, work the first row of stem stitch to the base of the left leaf. Work a second row with the same yarn, finishing one stitch into the left leaf stem. Finish the left leaf stem with a row of I.

Using F, work a row from the base to the top of the main stem. Change to J and work another row. Stitch a second row in J, finishing near the middle leaf. Change to F and work up to the tendril intersection. Change to H and work to the top of the main stem. Change to I and stitch along the main stem and then out and around the first curl of the tendril. Re-emerge where the tendril branches from the main stem and stitch to the top of the stem.

Using F, stitch from the main stem to the tip of the upper curl of the tendril. Beginning at the base of the upper curl, work the lower section of the tendril in G. Fill the space where the tendril meets the main stem with 1–2 stitches in G. Change to I and work 3–4 stitches along the lower half of the upper curl.

Flower

Embroider a line of split stitch along the outer line of one middle petal. Work blanket stitch from the next marked line and over the split stitch. Work the remaining two sections in the same manner. Repeat for the left petal.

Stitch the five rows of couching on the upper petals, working from the darkest pink row to the lightest. Work a row of Palestrina stitch around each upper petal. Embroider the seed stitches next.

Work nine rows of stem stitch for the bottom half of the left lower petal and twelve rows for the lower half of the petal on the right hand side. Outline the upper half of these petals then work the French knots, grading from the darkest shades near the centre to the lightest shades near the petal tips.

Outline the centre with split stitch. Fill the entire area with satin stitch, covering the split stitch outline. Overlay the satin stitches with a lattice of diagonal straight stitches. Couch the intersections of the lattice with tiny straight stitches.

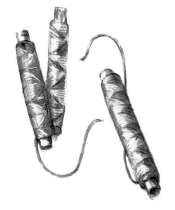

CREWEL SAMPLER

Requirements

Appletons 2 ply crewel wool
A = 151 ultra lt mid blue
B = 152 vy lt mid blue
C = 153 lt mid blue
D = 154 mid blue
E = 155 med mid blue
F = 341 ultra lt mid olive green
G = 343 lt mid olive green
H = 344 mid olive green
I = 345 med mid olive green
J = 351 ultra lt grey green
K = 751 ultra lt rose pink
L = 752 vy lt rose pink
M = 753 lt rose pink
N = 754 med rose pink
O = 755 rose pink
P = 756 dk rose pink
Q = 876 pastel blue

Embroidery key

All embroidery is worked with two strands unless otherwise specified.

Middle leaf

Centre = H (cretan stitch)

Upper outline = D and G (stem stitch)

Lower outline = E and H (stem stitch)

Right leaf

Lower section = F, G, H and I (coral stitch)

Outside of upper section = F, G and I (stem stitch)

Inside of upper section = C, D and E (1 strand, stem stitch)

Left leaf

Upper section = F, G, H, I and J (coral stitch)

Outside of lower section = G, I and J (stem stitch)

Inside of lower section = A, D and E (1 strand, stem stitch)

Stems and tendril

Main stem = F, G, H, I and J (stem stitch)

Stem to left leaf = G and I (stem stitch)

Tendril = F, G and I (stem stitch)

Flower

Middle right petal = L, N and O
(split stitch, blanket stitch)

Middle left petal = K, M and N
(split stitch, blanket stitch)

Upper right petal = K, L, M, O and P
(1 strand, couching), P (Palestrina stitch),
B, C, D and E (1–2 strands, seed stitch)

Upper left petal = K, L, M, N and O (1 strand,
couching), O (Palestrina stitch), A, B, C and D
(1–2 strands, seed stitch)

Lower right petal = L, M, N, O and P (stem stitch),
B, C, D and E (1 strand, French knot, 1 wrap)

Lower left petal = K, L, M, N, O and P (stem stitch),
A, B, C and D (1 strand, French knot, 1 wrap)

Centre = B (1 strand, split stitch, satin stitch),
N and Q (1 strand, trellis couching)

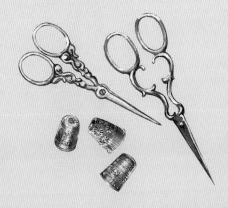

ROSE BOUQUET
by Bronwen Rossiter

Eight ruby roses are surrounded with eight long-stemmed rosebuds to form this glorious bouquet. A narrow ribbon, matching the richness of the roses, gently ties the arrangement.

Order of work

Embroider the roses first, beginning each one from the centre and working outwards. The inner petals of the rosebuds are stitched next, followed by the outer petals. Embroider all stems and detached chain leaves with the green wool. Add the fly stitch leaves and finally the bow, working the loops and ties before the bow knot.

Requirements

DMC tapestry wool
A = 7139 dk garnet
B = 7398 Brunswick green
C = 7758 deep rose
DMC stranded cotton
D = 502 blue-green
**Toray Sillook ribbon yarn
3.6mm (³⁄₁₆″) wide**
E = 25cm (10″) no. 422 wine

Embroidery key

All embroidery is worked with one strand unless otherwise specified.

Roses

Centre = A (3 straight stitches)
Inner petals = A (2 bullion knots, 6 wraps)
Outer petals = C (3 bullion knots, 8 wraps)

Rosebuds

Inner petal = A (bullion knot, 6 wraps)
Outer petals = C (2 bullion knots, 4 wraps)

Stems and leaves

Stems = B (straight stitch)
Large leaves = B (detached chain)
Small leaves = D (2 strands, fly stitch)

Bow

Loops = E (detached chain)
Ties = E (2 straight stitches)
Knot = E (2 straight stitches)

This design uses
Detached chain, bullion knot,
fly stitch, straight stitch

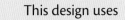

DOGWOOD ROSE
by Margo Fanning

Reminiscent of the blooms from Granny's garden, the single open rose, buds and leaves are created using soft shading.

This design uses

Back stitch, blanket stitch,
French knot, granitos,
long and short stitch, rope stitch,
satin stitch, soft shading,
straight stitch

Order of work

Rose

Embroider all the petals from the outer edge towards the centre. Work the first row in blanket stitch and the remaining rows in long and short stitch. When stitching the lower petals, work the blanket stitch so the 'purls' are towards the centre. This gives the appearance of the petals curling over.

For the centre, work a French knot in D and surround it with four tiny straight stitches. Change to B and mass French knots around the middle stitches.

Rosebuds

Stitch the petals of the four buds in satin stitch. Add a granitos calyx to each bud.

Foliage

Work the stems first and then the leaves in satin stitch. Place straight stitches over the satin stitches to achieve the variegated look of the leaves. Embroider straight stitches over the buds for the new foliage.

Requirements

Appletons 2 ply crewel wool
A = 242 lt olive green
B = 243 olive green
C = 311 ultra lt brown olive
D = 333 lt drab green
E = 752 vy lt rose pink
F = 991 white
Paterna Persian yarn
G = D511 dk verdigris
**Kacoonda hand dyed medium
embroidery wool**
H = 108 variegated rose

Embroidery key

*All embroidery is worked with one strand
unless otherwise specified.*

Rose

Petals = H (blanket stitch, long and short stitch),
E and F (long and short stitch)

Centre = D (straight stitch, French knot,
1 wrap), C (French knot, 1 wrap)

Rosebuds

Petals = H (satin stitch)

Calyx = B and G blended together
(1 strand of each, granitos)

New foliage = B and G blended together
(1 strand of each, straight stitch)

Leaves and stems

Leaves = B and G (satin stitch, straight stitch)

Leaf veins = G (back stitch)

Stem on left = A (rope stitch)

Stems on right = G (rope stitch)

JACOBEAN CIRCLET
by Margery Opie

This stylised flower echoes those seen in traditional crewel embroidery designs. A circlet of intertwined stems, leaves and buds surrounds the flower.

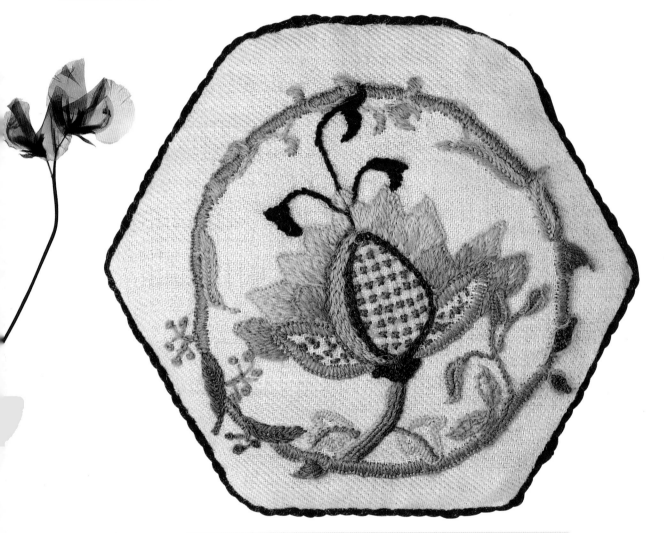

This design uses

Blanket stitch, chain stitch, coral stitch, detached blanket stitch,
French knot, fly stitch, long and short stitch, outline stitch,
satin stitch, seed stitch, soft shading, stem stitch, straight stitch,
trellis couching, twisted detached blanket stitch, whipped stem stitch

Order of work

Begin at the centre of the flower with the section of trellis couching. Outline this section with chain stitch and work the rows of chain stitch on the left hand side to complete the petal. Embroider the blue petals on either side in blanket stitch and fill their centres with seed stitch.

The yellow petals are stitched next, starting from the centre top petal and working down to the lowest petals on either side. Add the scarlet tendrils to the top of the flower in satin and stem stitch.

Stitch the calyx with French knots and then the stem with four rows of whipped stem stitch. Add a leaf to each side of the stem.

Work the leaves and buds within the circlet, followed by the leaves, buds and flowers on the outside. Finally embroider the green blanket stitch border.

Trailing Vine, Inspirations 10

Requirements

Appletons 2 ply crewel wool

A = 255 dk grass green
B = 335 med drab green
C = 337 dk drab green
D = 341 ultra lt mid olive green
E = 343 lt mid olive green
F = 344 mid olive green
G = 345 med mid olive green
H = 504 dk scarlet
I = 546 early English green
J = 691 ultra lt honeysuckle yellow
K = 692 vy lt honeysuckle yellow
L = 694 med honeysuckle yellow
M = 695 honeysuckle yellow
N = 742 vy lt bright China blue
O = 744 med bright China blue
P = 745 bright China blue
Q = 754 med rose pink
R = 755 rose pink

Embroidery key

All embroidery is worked with two strands.

Flower

Centre petal = C, D and G (chain stitch), D and G (trellis couching)

Side petals = O (blanket stitch), P (seed stitch)

Upper petals = J, K, L and M (long and short stitch, stem stitch)

Tendrils = H (stem stitch, satin stitch)

Calyx = C (French knot, 1 wrap)

Stem = B, D, E and F (whipped stem stitch)

Leaves = F (whipped stem stitch), K (blanket stitch)

Circlet – Pink flowers

Flowers = Q or R (French knot, 2 wraps)

Stems = F (stem stitch), Q or R (straight stitch)

Blue buds

Buds = N or P (satin stitch)

Stems = D (stem stitch)

Yellow buds

Buds = L (twisted detached blanket stitch), E or F (detached blanket stitch or twisted detached blanket stitch)

Stems = F (stem stitch)

Leaves

Yellow leaves = L (coral stitch)

Pale green leaves = D (fly stitch)

Bright green leaves = A (fly stitch, outline stitch)

Two-tone leaves = D (outline stitch), I (French knot, 1 wrap)

Border = E (blanket stitch)

RIBBONS AND ROSES
by Donna Stevens

Soft pink spider web roses, surrounded by tiny forget-me-nots, delicate trails of pink buds and detached chain leaves, are tied with a flowing blue-violet ribbon.

This design uses

Back stitch, detached chain,
French knot, running stitch,
spider web rose

Order of work

Outline the ribbons in back stitch, beginning and ending near the flowers.

Stitch the roses next, using a different shade of pink for each one. Add a French knot for the centres.

Work the stems of the pink sprays in running stitch and embroider five pairs of detached chain flowers along each one.

Stitch the forget-me-nots next. Embroider a pink French knot in the centre and surround this with four blue French knots for the petals.

Finally, add tiny detached chain leaves among the roses and forget-me-nots.

Requirements

DMC stranded cotton
A = 3733 dusky rose
Gumnut Yarns 'Blossoms'
2 ply crewel wool
B = 093 vy lt dusky rose
C = 094 lt dusky rose
D = 095 dusky rose
E = 557 dk sea green
Gumnut Yarns 'Gemstones'
variegated 2 ply crewel wool
F = AZ4 lt blue-violet
G = AZ5 blue-violet

Embroidery key

All embroidery is worked with one strand unless otherwise specified.

Ribbons = F (back stitch)

Roses
Petals = B, C or D (spider web rose)
Centre = A (2 strands, French knot, 2 wraps)

Pink sprays
Flowers = D (detached chain)
Stems = E (running stitch)

Forget-me-nots
Petals = G (French knot, 1 wrap)
Centre = A (2 strands, French knot, 2 wraps)
Leaves = E (detached chain)

Pins and Needles, Inspirations 20

ROSE SPRAY
by Kris Richards

Two large roses are the centrepiece of this spray. Blue daisies and yellow French knot buds surround the roses. Dainty rosebuds and leaves complete the spray.

This design uses

Bullion knot, detached chain, fly stitch, French knot, straight stitch

Order of work

Using the darkest shade of pink, work the centre of each rose with two bullion knots. Change to the medium shade of pink and work the inner petals. Stitch the outer petals using the pale pink yarn.

Work the blue daisies in detached chain, adding a white French knot for each centre.

Stitch the large bullion rosebud and three smaller bullion buds next. Finish each one with one to two straight stitches at the tip of the petals and a fly stitch calyx.

Embroider the large light green leaves in fly stitch and the small dark green leaves in detached chain.

Fill in any gaps around the roses with yellow French knot buds.

Requirements

DMC broder médicis 1 ply wool
A = 8223 shell pink
B = 8119 lt plum
C = 8225 vy lt shell pink
D = 8402 avocado
E = 8405 vy lt sage green
Appletons 2 ply crewel wool
F = 991B bright white
G = 893 med hyacinth
Paterna Persian yarn
H = 715 vy lt mustard

Embroidery key

All embroidery is worked with one strand unless otherwise specified.

Roses

Centre = A (2 strands, 2 bullion knots, 6 wraps)

Inner petals = B (2 strands, 3 bullion knots, 10 wraps)

Outer petals = C (2 strands, 4–5 bullion knots, 10–12 wraps)

Large rosebud

Inner petals = A (2 strands, 2 bullion knots, 10 wraps)

Outer petals = C (2 strands, 2 bullion knots, 10 wraps)

Calyx = E (fly stitch)

Tip = E (1–2 straight stitches)

Small rosebuds

Inner petals = A (2 strands, bullion knot, 10 wraps)

Outer petals = C (2 strands, 2 bullion knots, 10 wraps)

Calyx = E (fly stitch)

Tip = E (1–2 straight stitches)

Daisies

Petals = G (3–5 detached chains)

Centre = F (French knot, 2 wraps)

French knot buds = H (French knot, 1 wrap)

Leaves = D (detached chain), E (fly stitch)

TOPIARY
by Kris Richards

Standing in a traditional terracotta pot, this elegant topiary is embroidered in soft shades of dusky pink, blue and lavender.

This design uses

Bullion knot, detached chain, fly stitch, French knot, stem stitch, straight stitch, wound rose

Order of work

Terracotta pot

Embroider the pot with horizontal rows of stem stitch. Outline the rim, sides and base with straight stitch and stem stitch.

Topiary

Using the biscuit brown yarn, work two rows of stem stitch side by side for the trunk of the topiary.

Using the lighter pink yarn, embroider the seven wound roses first. Add a French knot to the centre of each one.

Work the lavender flowers around the outer edge of the topiary with single bullion knots. Finish each one with a fly stitch around the base.

Using the blue-violet yarn, work the groups of French knot flowers and buds among the roses and lavender. Stitch the leaves in detached chain.

Requirements

DMC broder médicis 1 ply wool
A = 8119 lt plum
B = 8225 vy lt shell pink
C = 8332 blue-violet
D = 8400 golden olive
E = 8402 avocado
Appletons 2 ply crewel wool
F = 763 lt biscuit brown
G = 764 biscuit brown
H = 765 med biscuit brown
Paterna Persian yarn
I = D137 basil
J = 344 ultra lt periwinkle

Embroidery key

All embroidery is worked with one strand.

Terracotta pot

Pot = H (stem stitch)

Outline = G (stem stitch, straight stitch)

Roses

Petals = B (wound rose)

Centre = A (French knot, 1 wrap)

Lavender

Flowers = I (bullion knot, 6 wraps)

Calyx = E (fly stitch)

French knot flowers = J (French knot, 1 wrap)

Buds = C (French knot, 1 wrap)

Leaves = D (detached chain)

Trunk = F (stem stitch)

Wound rose

Insert a spare needle into the fabric to form the framework around which a rose can be wound. After it has been wound, couch it in place to secure it to the fabric.

A FLORAL TOUCH
by Jan Kerton

A pretty pink blossom, buds, sprigs of lavender and tiny forget-me-nots make up this diminutive spray.

This design uses
Detached chain, fly stitch, French knot, granitos, straight stitch

Order of work

Pink blossom and buds

Stitch the blossom, followed by the three buds. For each bud, work a granitos using 7–9 straight stitches. Overlay this with 1–2 straight stitches for petal markings. Surround the bud with a green fly stitch, extending the anchoring stitch towards the blossom. Complete the sepals with 1–2 straight stitches over the lower half of the bud. Add two detached chain leaves near the blossom.

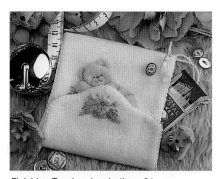

Finishing Touches, Inspirations 21

Lavender

For each sprig of lavender, stitch two pairs of detached chains, angling the tips of the stitches in each pair away from each other. Add a single detached chain to the end of each sprig.

Beginning just below the first pair of flowers, embroider a pair of straight stitches that share the same hole in the fabric near the base of the flowers. Angle the stitches so they follow the same direction as the flowers.

Forget-me-nots

Embroider a single yellow French knot for the centre of each flower. Surround this with a circle of French knots for the petals.

Requirements

Appletons 2 ply crewel wool
A = 751 ultra lt rose pink
B = 886 pastel blue-violet
DMC broder médicis 1 ply wool
C = 8224 lt shell pink
D = 8328 vy lt yellow
E = 8369 pistachio
Gumnut yarns 'Gemstones' variegated 2 ply crewel wool
F = A2 lt lavender
DMC no. 8 perlé cotton
G = 712 cream

Embroidery key

All embroidery is worked with one strand unless otherwise specified.

Blossom

Petals = A (granitos)

Petal markings = C (straight stitch)

Divisions between petals = E (straight stitch)

Centre = D blended with E (1 strand of each, French knot, 1 wrap)

Leaves = E (detached chain)

Buds

Petals = A (granitos)

Petal markings = C (straight stitch)

Sepals = E (fly stitch, straight stitch)

Lavender

Flowers = F (detached chain)

Sepals = E (straight stitch)

Forget-me-nots

Petals = B (French knot, 2 wraps)

Centre = D (French knot, 2 wraps)

GARLAND OF SPRING FLOWERS
by Carolyn Pearce

This exquisite garland of flowers, in soft muted tones, exudes old world charm.

This design uses

Colonial knot, couching, detached chain, fly stitch, French knot, granitos, smocker's knot, stem stitch, straight stitch, twisted detached chain, whipping

Order of work

Apple blossoms

Embroider the five apple blossoms following the step-by-step instructions on page 78.

Large roses

Stitch the roses, beginning at the outer edge with the lightest shade and grading to the darkest shade in the centre. Keep the rounds of stitching close together.

Large buds and leaves

Follow the instructions on page 79 to work the large gold buds.

Stitch the petal of each large cream bud in the same manner as a blossom petal and finish in the same manner as the gold buds.

Embroider the fly stitch leaves in the mohair yarn.

White violets

Stitch a granitos for each petal, stitching the two upper petals before the lower petals. Embroider a fly stitch around the tip of each petal and a straight stitch over the top. Add three tightly clustered colonial knots for the centres.

Work a single straight stitch radiating from the centre on each of the three lower petals.

Ribbon roses and rosebuds

Embroider the petals of the roses in stem stitches which spiral inwards, finishing with a colonial knot at the centre. For each bud, stitch four overlapping straight stitches, allowing the ribbon to twist.

Add a calyx and stamens to the four buds in the lower section of the design. Work the stems, ribbon leaves and remaining fly stitch leaves.

White forget-me-nots

Work the centre and surround this with five colonial knots for the petals. Stitch pairs of detached chains with long anchoring stitches for the leaves.

GARLAND OF SPRING FLOWERS

Requirements

Appletons 2 ply crewel wool
A = 351 ultra lt grey green
B = 472 vy lt autumn yellow
C = 841 vy lt heraldic gold
D = 851 custard yellow
E = 882 cream
F = 991 white

Paterna Persian yarn
G = 716 ultra lt mustard

**Gumnut Yarns 'Daisies'
1 ply fine wool**
H = 645 khaki

**Littlewood Fleece Yarns
2 ply gossamer mohair**
I = pink kangaroo paw
J = orange/brown

DMC stranded cotton
K = 676 lt old gold
L = 921 copper
M = 3051 dk green-grey
N = 3721 dk shell pink

Weeks Dye Works silk thread
O = 1201 putty

Rajmahal Art silk
P = 45 baby camel
Q = 311 Fresco oil
R = 421 green earth
S = 841 gilded bronze

Kanagawa 380 denier silk thread
T = 114 lt sage green

**Vintage Ribbons silk ribbon 4mm
(³⁄₁₆″) wide**
U = 1m (1yd 3½″) pine needles

**Kacoonda silk ribbon
4mm (³⁄₁₆″) wide**
V = 2m (2yd 7″) no. 4 blush

Ribbon floss 4mm (³⁄₁₆″) wide
W = 1.5m (1yd 23″) white

Embroidery key

*All embroidery is worked with one strand
unless otherwise specified.*

Apple blossoms

Petals = E (2 strands, granitos)
Between petals = H (straight stitch)
Petal tips = A (fly stitch, straight stitch)
Centre = B, L, M and N blended together
(1 strand of each, colonial knot)
Petal markings = T (straight stitch)

Rose 1

Petals = G (stem stitch), D and J
(2 strands, stem stitch)
Centre = J (2 strands, colonial knot)

Rose 2

Petals = C, D and J
(2 strands, stem stitch)
Centre = J (2 strands, colonial knot)

Large gold buds

Inner petal = D (2 strands, granitos)
Outer petals = C and E (2 strands, granitos)
Calyx = H and Q (straight stitch, granitos)
Stamens = Q (fly stitch)
Stem = H (couching), Q (whipping)

Large cream buds

Petal = E (2 strands, granitos)
Calyx = H and Q (straight stitch, granitos)
Stamens = Q (fly stitch)
Stem = H (couching), Q (whipping)

Large leaves = I (fly stitch, smocker's knot),
O and S (2 strands, fly stitch, smocker's knot)

White violets

Petals = F (granitos)
Petal tips = R (fly stitch, straight stitch)
Centre = 1 strand of N blended with 2 strands of P
(colonial knot)
Petal markings = P (straight stitch)

Ribbon roses

Petals = V (stem stitch)
Centre = V (colonial knot)
Buds = V (straight stitch)
Calyx on lower buds = O (fly stitch)
Stamens on lower buds = O (straight stitch)
Leaves = U (twisted detached chain),
O (straight stitch, smocker's knot)
Stem = O (2 strands, stem stitch)

White forget-me-nots

Centre = 5 strands of K blended with 1 strand of O
(colonial knot)
Petals = W (colonial knot)
Leaves = O (2 strands, detached chain)

RING OF ROSES
by Kris Richards

Palest pink wound roses nestle among clusters of daisies in this charming circlet.

This design uses

Detached chain, French knot, granitos, wound rose

Order of work

Work the petals of the wound roses first, using the pale pink yarn. Stitch a French knot in the centre of each one.

Using detached chain, embroider the blue daisies, followed by the white daisies. Work a yellow French knot in the centre of the white daisies.

Stitch detached chain leaves around the roses and daisies using the light green yarn. With the dark green yarn, work detached chain leaves around the clusters to fill in any spaces.

To link the clusters, work one or two granitos.

Requirements

Appletons 2 ply crewel wool
A = 252 lt grass green
B = 851 custard yellow
C = 893 med hyacinth
D = 991B bright white
Paterna Persian yarn
E = 492 med flesh
F = 641 drab khaki green
G = 924 pale wood rose

Embroidery key

All embroidery is worked with one strand unless otherwise specified.

Roses

Petals = E (wound rose)

Centre = G (2 strands, French knot, 1 wrap)

Blue daisies = C (detached chain)

White daisies

Petals = D (detached chain)

Centre = B (French knot, 1 wrap)

Leaves = A and F (detached chain)

Spots = E (granitos)

FOXGLOVES
by Margo Fanning

Shades of pale pink and rich plum are used to fill the trumpets of this majestic foxglove spire.

Order of work

Flowers

Stitch the lips of the three lower flowers first, using long and short blanket stitch for the lower sections and blanket stitch for the upper sections and sides. Fill the trumpets with long and short stitch. Work straight stitches over the top to help blend the colours. Stitch the spots inside the trumpets. Work two straight stitches and a French knot for each one.

Work the lips of the middle flowers using stem stitch for the upper edge and long and short blanket stitch for the sides and lower sections. Fill the trumpets in the same manner as the lower flowers.

Stitch the petals of the buds next.

Stems, calyxes and leaves

Work all the stems and then the calyxes of the buds and flowers. At the base of the plant, embroider the two outer leaves in satin stitch and the middle leaf in long and short stitch. Work the vein on the left leaf. Add the leaves at the tip of the main stem last.

This design uses

Back stitch, blanket stitch, French knot, long and short blanket stitch, long and short stitch, rope stitch, satin stitch, soft shading, stem stitch, straight stitch

Hints on working with wool

• When embroidering, work with an even tension but one that is slightly looser than for other thread embroidery.

• To help prevent the yarn becoming worn, use short lengths approximately 40cm (16") long. Choose a needle which will make a large enough hole in the fabric for the yarn to pass through easily.

• If the ply of the yarn unravels, gently twist the yarns with your fingers to re-ply it. If the yarn appears to be over twisted, let the needle dangle freely for a few seconds and allow the yarn to settle back to its original twist.

• If working on canvas, cover the edges with masking tape or similar as the rough edges tend to catch and snag the yarn.

Requirements

Appletons 2 ply crewel wool

A = 144 dull rose pink
B = 145 med dull rose pink
C = 149 ultra dk dull rose pink
D = 243 olive green
E = 342 vy lt mid olive green
F = 344 mid olive green
G = 351 ultra lt grey green
H = 542 vy lt early English green
I = 752 vy lt rose pink
J = 757 vy dk rose pink
K = 759 ultra dk rose pink
L = 992 off-white

Paterna Persian yarn

M = 441 dk golden brown
N = D511 dk verdigris

Embroidery key

*All embroidery is worked with one strand
unless otherwise specified.*

Lower flowers

Lip = I (blanket stitch, long and short blanket stitch)

Outer trumpet = A, B, C, J, K and L
(long and short stitch, straight stitch)

Inner trumpet = A, B, I and J
(long and short stitch, straight stitch)

Spots = K and L (straight stitch),
J (French knot, 1 wrap)

Sepals = D, E, F, L and N (satin stitch, straight stitch)

Middle flowers on right

Lip = I (stem stitch, long and short blanket stitch)

Outer trumpet = A, B, I and J
(long and short stitch, straight stitch)

Inner trumpet = A, B and J
(long and short stitch, straight stitch)

Sepals = D and H (satin stitch, straight stitch)

Middle flower on left

Lip = A (blanket stitch, stem stitch)

Outer trumpet = B, J and K (long and short stitch,
straight stitch)

Inner trumpet = K (straight stitch)

Sepals = E and N (satin stitch, straight stitch)

Upper middle flower on left

Lip = A (blanket stitch, stem stitch,
long and short stitch)

Outer trumpet = A, B, and K
(long and short stitch, straight stitch)

Inner trumpet = C (straight stitch)

Sepals = E and H (satin stitch, straight stitch)

Bud on right

Petals = A and B (blanket stitch, long and short stitch)

Sepals = D (satin stitch), F (long and short stitch)

Middle bud

Petals = A (blanket stitch)

Sepals = D and H (satin stitch, straight stitch)

Bud on left

Petal = A (long and short stitch)

Lip = H (blanket stitch)

Markings on lip = I (straight stitch)

Sepals = G (blanket stitch, long
and short stitch), F (satin stitch,
straight stitch)

Stem

Lower section = D and N (long and short stitch),
M (straight stitch)

Middle section = F (long and short stitch)

Upper section = E and F (rope stitch)

Leaves

Lower leaves = D and M (satin stitch),
D and E (long and short stitch)

Vein on lower left leaf = E (2 strands, back stitch)

Upper leaves = E and F (straight stitch)

Long and short blanket stitch

As the name suggests, long and short blanket stitch
comprises stitches of varying lengths. It can be used
in straight lines or scallops as a decorative edge.
When used to fill a shape, the loops define the outline.

Rule two parallel lines on the fabric to help you
position the stitches correctly.

PANSY BOUQUET
by Carolyn Pearce

The exquisite spray showcases a stumpwork pansy and buds
sprinkled with violets, forget-me-nots and leaves.

This design uses
Beading, chain stitch, colonial knot, detached chain, fly stitch, granitos,
long and short blanket stitch, long and short stitch, ruching, running stitch,
smocker's knot, soft shading, straight stitch, whipping

Order of work

Refer to the pattern on page 125 and the list of materials required on page 100.

Padding

Cut out the petals for the pansy and two larger buds from the felt. Secure them to the fabric in the order they are numbered. Petals 2 and 5 of the pansy and one petal of the large buds each have two layers of padding.

Pansy

Embroider the upper petals (marked 'u' on the pattern) from the outer edge towards the centre. Work the remaining petals in the same manner. Overlay the petals with long straight stitches of differing lengths which radiate from the middle. Stitch two colonial knots for the centre.

Centre bud

Work a granitos of five straight stitches for the petal. Add three more straight stitches over the top. Embroider a fly stitch around the tip and add 2–4 straight stitches over the petal.

Right hand bud

Embroider the lower petal and then the upper petal. Work the highlights over the previous stitching. Embroider the sepals in fly stitch.

Left hand bud

Stitch this bud in the same manner as the right hand bud.

Violets

Work a granitos for each petal, stitching the two upper petals before the lower petals. Embroider a fly stitch around the tip of each petal and a straight stitch over the top. Add three tightly clustered colonial knots for each centre.

Forget-me-nots

Cut the ribbon into 9cm (3½") lengths. Measure in 2cm (¾") from each end and mark. Between the marks, mark the ribbon at 1cm (⅜") intervals. Work tiny running stitches following diagram 1. Pull up the running stitches to gather (or ruche) the ribbon.

Using the gathering thread, join A to B (see diagrams 1 and 2). Take the ribbon tails to the back of the fabric and secure. Work a colonial knot for the centre.

Leaves

Work large fly stitch leaves around the pansy, detached chain leaves near the forget-me-nots and fly stitch leaves near the violets.

Scattered buds

Secure groups of four beads in a 'Y' shape around the outer edge of the bouquet.

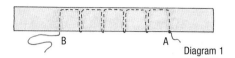

Diagram 1

Diagram 2

Bouquet of Flowers, Inspirations 29

99

PANSY BOUQUET

Requirements

5 × 20cm (2 × 8″) wide piece of felt

Appletons 2 ply crewel wool
A = 104 med purple
B = 841 vy lt heraldic gold
DMC broder médicis 1 ply wool
C = 8405 vy lt sage
D = 8412 moss
E = 8420 med yellow-green
Paterna Persian yarn
F = D127 med basil
**Gumnut Yarns 'Buds' shaded
perlé silk**
G = 647 vy dk khaki
Torokina Yarns hand dyed wool
H = 221 lt lilac
I = 222 med lilac
J = 223 dk lilac
Torokina silk
K = 440 fresh green
**Littlewood Fleece Yarns 2 ply
gossamer mohair**
L = sage green
M = soft apple green
DMC stranded cotton
N = 223 lt shell pink
O = 327 vy dk lavender
P = 554 lt violet
Q = 745 vy lt yellow
R = 793 med cornflower blue
S = 3721 dk shell pink
T = 3726 dk antique mauve
U = 3740 dk antique violet
V = 3746 dk blue-violet
**Minnamurra variegated
stranded cotton**
W = 110 purple/gold
YLI silk floss
X = 181 gold beige

Madeira Decora stranded rayon
Y = 1557 dk olive
Rajmahal Art silk
Z = 45 baby camel
AA = 421 green earth
Marabout chenille
BB = 4157 fiesta
YLI silk ribbon 4mm (³⁄₁₆″) wide
CC = 65cm (25½″)
no. 90 vy lt antique blue
Mill Hill glass seed beads
DD = 00206 violet

Embroidery key

*All embroidery is worked with one strand
unless otherwise specified.*

Pansy

Upper petals = I (long and short blanket stitch,
long and short stitch), J (long and short stitch)

Middle and lower petals = H (long and short blanket
stitch), B (long and short stitch), A (straight stitch)

Highlights on upper petals = N, O, Q, R and W
(straight stitch)

Highlights on middle and lower petals = O, P, Q, R, T
and W (straight stitch)

Centre = BB (colonial knot)

Centre bud

Petal = H (2 strands, granitos),
V (fly stitch, straight stitch)

Sepals = G (fly stitch, smocker's knot)

Stem = E (stem stitch), AA (whipping)

Right hand bud

Lower petal = I (long and short stitch)

Upper petal = B (long and short stitch)

Petal highlights = V and AA (straight stitch)

Sepals = G (fly stitch, smocker's knot)

Stem = D (chain stitch), G (whipping)

Left hand bud

Lower petal = H (long and short stitch)

Upper petal = I (long and short stitch)

Petal highlights = V and AA (straight stitch)

Sepals = K (fly stitch, smocker's knot)

Stem = C (chain stitch), K (whipping)

Violets

Petals = F (granitos), U (fly stitch, straight stitch)

Centre = 1 strand of S blended with
2 strands of Z (colonial knot)

Forget-me-nots

Petals = CC (ruching)

Centre = X (6 strands, colonial knot)

Leaves

Large leaves = K, L or M (fly stitch, smocker's knot)

Small leaves = AA (detached chain), Y (fly stitch)

Scattered buds = DD (beading)

SHASTA DAISY
by Margo Fanning

These cheerful white daisies are so realistically reproduced it is difficult to tell them from those in the corner of a cottage garden.

Requirements

Appletons 2 ply crewel wool
A = 151 ultra lt mid blue
B = 242 lt olive green
C = 692 vy lt honeysuckle yellow
D = 694 med honeysuckle yellow
E = 841 vy lt heraldic gold
F = 842 lt heraldic gold
G = 991 white

Embroidery key

All embroidery is worked with one strand.

Daisies

Petals = A and G (long and short stitch)

Centre of left daisy = C, D and E
(French knot, 1–2 wraps)

Centre of middle daisy = C, D and E
(French knot, 1–2 wraps)

Centre of right daisy = C, D and F
(French knot, 1–2 wraps)

Stem = B (rope stitch)

Leaves = B (satin stitch)

This design uses

French knot, long and short stitch, rope stitch, satin stitch, soft shading

Order of work

Stitch the petals, working from the outer edge to the centre for each one. Fill the centre with closely packed French knots. Use the darker yellows in the lower section of each centre and the lighter yellows in the upper area. Mix some knots of each colour so the colour changes are more natural.

Embroider the stems with narrow rope stitch and then work each leaf with two rows of satin stitch.

PRIMROSE
by Margo Fanning

The primrose is the essence of spring with its endearing little flowers.

This design uses

Blanket stitch, bullion knot,
chain stitch, colonial knot,
long and short blanket stitch,
long and short stitch, rope stitch,
satin stitch, split stitch, stem stitch,
straight stitch, whipped stem stitch,
woven filling stitch

Order of work

Primrose

Embroider the petals, beginning with the blanket stitch edging. Blend long and short stitches into the blanket stitches. Work the petal markings over the previous stitching. Add three colonial knots to the centre of each flower.

Work the petals of the buds in the same manner as the flower petals. Stitch the calyxes of the flowers and buds. When working the calyxes on the buds, blend the stitches with those of the petals.

Stitch the leaves in satin stitch, working one side at a time. Place straight stitches of varying shades over the leaves to help blend the colours. Work the veins last.

Finally, embroider the stems, using the photograph as a guide to colour placement.

Snail

Stitch the body first. To work the shell, stitch a line of chain stitch through the middle of the spiral for padding. Cover this with blanket stitch, spiralling from the centre outwards. Embroider a bullion knot with a colonial knot at the end for each feeler.

Requirements

Appletons 2 ply crewel wool
A = 183 lt chocolate
B = 294 Jacobean green
C = 311 ultra lt brown olive
D = 353 lt grey green
E = 355 grey green
F = 541 ultra lt early English green
G = 551 ultra lt bright yellow
H = 552 vy lt bright yellow
I = 855 dull gold
J = 872 rich cream

Kacoonda medium variegated wool
K = 200 clay
L = 201 fawn

Paterna Persian yarn
M = 643 lt khaki green

Embroidery key

All embroidery is worked with one strand unless otherwise specified.

Centre flower
Upper petals = J (long and short blanket stitch, long and short stitch)

Lower petals = I (long and short blanket stitch), G (long and short stitch)

Petal markings = C and G (straight stitch)

Centre = M (colonial knot)

Upper right flower
Petals = J (long and short blanket stitch, long and short stitch), G (long and short stitch)

Petal markings = C and H (straight stitch)

Centre = M (colonial knot)

Calyx = F and M blended together (1 strand of each, straight stitch)

Lower left flower
Petals = I and J (long and short blanket stitch, long and short stitch)

Petal markings = C (straight stitch)

Centre = M (colonial knot)

Calyx = F (long and short stitch)

Lower right flower
Petals = I and J (long and short blanket stitch, long and short stitch)

Petal markings = C (straight stitch)

Centre = M (colonial knot)

Calyx = F and M blended together (1 strand of each, long and short stitch)

Side-view flower
Petals = J (long and short blanket stitch, long and short stitch)

Petal markings = C (straight stitch)

Calyx = F and M blended together (1 strand of each, long and short stitch)

Buds on left
Petals = H (long and short blanket stitch, long and short stitch)

Calyx = F and M blended together or D and E blended together (1 strand of each, long and short stitch)

Buds on right
Petals = I (long and short blanket stitch, long and short stitch)

Calyx = F and M blended together (1 strand of each, long and short stitch)

Stems and leaves
Leaves = B, D, E, F and M (satin stitch, straight stitch)

Leaf veins = M (split stitch)

Stems = A (whipped stem stitch), F and M blended together (1 strand of each, rope stitch or stem stitch)

Snail
Body = A blended with L (1 strand of each, woven filling stitch)

Shell padding = K (2 strands, chain stitch)

Shell = K (blanket stitch)

Feelers = A (bullion knot, 6–8 wraps, colonial knot)

DAISY SPRAY
by Annie Humphris

Three pretty pink daisies are mixed with pink and cream buds to create this circular spray.

This design uses

Detached chain, fly stitch,
French knot, granitos,
running stitch, straight stitch

Order of work

Stitch the large daisy in the centre first,
working from the middle outwards.
Embroider the small daisies next. Work
a detached chain for the inside of each
petal and surround it with a second
detached chain.

Begin each pink bud with a granitos
of eight straight stitches. Add the
calyxes, highlights and stamens. Stitch
the cream buds in the same manner.
Work the stems and fronds last.

Requirements

Appletons 2 ply crewel wool
A = 141 ultra lt dull rose pink
B = 142 vy lt dull rose pink
Anchor Marlitt stranded rayon
C = 872 lt putty groundings
Anchor stranded cotton
D = 858 lt fern green

Embroidery key

*All embroidery is worked with one strand
unless otherwise specified.*

Large daisy

Petals = A blended with C
(1 strand of each, detached chain)

Inner centre = C
(2 strands, French knot, 1 wrap)

Outer centre = B
(4 French knots, 2 wraps)

Small daisies

Inside of petals = C (detached chain)

Outside of petals = A (detached chain)

Pink buds

Petals = A (granitos)

Petal highlights = C (straight stitch)

Stamens = D (fly stitch)

Upper calyx = D (detached chain,
straight stitch)

Lower calyx = A blended with C
(1 strand of each, French knot, 1 wrap)

Stem = D (straight stitch)

Cream buds

Petals = C (granitos)

Stamens = D (fly stitch)

Calyx = D (detached chain,
French knot, 2 wraps)

Stem = D (2 strands, straight stitch)

Fronds

Stems = D (running stitch)

Leaves = D (detached chain)

BOW
by Kris Richards

This neatly tied classic bow has a central spray of roses, rosebuds and French knot buds. A large rose is placed over the centre of the bow, while the rosebuds, leaves and buds are worked around this central rose.

This design uses

Bullion knot, detached chain, fly stitch, French knot, stem stitch, straight stitch

Order of work

Using the cornflower blue yarn, work the bow loops in stem stitch and then the ribbon tails.

Embroider two bullion knots for the centre of the large rose using the darkest shade of pink yarn. Change to the medium pink and stitch the three inner petals. Stitch the five outer petals using the lightest shade of pink.

Work the rosebuds next, following the embroidery key for colour changes.

Using the sage green yarn, embroider the leaves in detached chain.

Add the French knot buds around the rose and rosebuds.

Requirements

DMC broder médicis 1 ply wool
A = 8405 vy lt sage green
Appletons 2 ply crewel wool
B = 461 vy lt cornflower blue
C = 751 ultra lt rose pink
D = 754 med rose pink
Gumnut Yarns 'Blossoms'
2 ply crewel wool
E = 850 vy pale baby pink
Gumnut Yarns 'Daisies'
1 ply crewel wool
F = 624 soft green

Embroidery key

All embroidery is worked with one strand unless otherwise specified.

Bow

Loops = B (stem stitch)

Tails = B (stem stitch)

Rose

Centre = D (2 strands, 2 bullion knots, 6 wraps)

Inner petals = C (2 strands, 3 bullion knots, 10 wraps)

Outer petals = E (5 bullion knots, 10 wraps)

Large rosebuds

Centre = D (2 bullion knots, 6–8 wraps)

Petals = C (2 bullion knots, 8–10 wraps)

Calyx = A (fly stitch)

Small rosebuds

Centre = C or D (bullion knot, 6–8 wraps)

Petals = D or E (2 bullion knots, 8–10 wraps)

Calyx = A (fly stitch)

Leaves = A (detached chain, straight stitch)

French knot buds = F (2 strands, French knot, 2 wraps)

ROCKING HORSE
by Kris Richards

This endearing rocking horse is created with subtly shaded thread painting and embellished with ribbons, roses and buds. The dainty rocker and saddle are also decorated with roses and buds.

This design uses

Bullion knot, detached chain, granitos, French knot, long and short stitch, satin stitch, soft shading, split stitch, stem stitch, straight stitch

Order of work

Horse

Stitch the head and body first, followed by the mane and tail. Add the ear and hooves next.

Work a granitos of three straight stitches for the eye. Add a longer straight stitch at the top to extend the curve.

Outline the mouth and chin with split stitches.

Saddle and blanket

Outline the saddle with three rows of stem stitch and the scallops of the blanket with two rows of stem stitch. Use satin stitch to fill the scallops and long and short stitch for the saddle area.

Rocker

Work the pink band with two rows of stem stitch. Fill the outer section with rows of baby blue stem stitch. Stitch the middle section in the same manner using the cream yarn. Add highlights to the edge with the cream yarn.

Bridle and reins

Embroider parallel rows of stem stitch for the bridle and reins, stitching more rows in the wider sections.

Flowers

Stitch three bullion roses on the rocker, two on the saddle and one on the bridle. Embroider the rosebuds on the reins and saddle at the positions indicated on the pattern. Work partial daisies below the roses. Sprinkle tiny buds and leaves around the roses and rosebuds.

Rocker markings

After the flowers are complete, work three blue granitos on each side of the spray in the middle of the rocker.

Requirements

Appletons 2 ply crewel wool
A = 741 ultra lt bright china blue
B = 761 ultra lt biscuit brown
C = 762 vy lt biscuit brown
D = 764 biscuit brown
E = 876 pastel blue
F = 882 cream
G = 993 black
DMC broder médicis 1 ply wool
H = 8225 vy lt shell pink
DMC stranded cotton
I = 223 lt shell pink
J = 224 vy lt shell pink
K = 225 ultra lt shell pink
L = 3024 vy lt Jacobean green
M = 3743 vy lt antique violet
N = 3756 lt baby blue

Embroidery key

All embroidery is worked with one strand unless otherwise specified.

Horse

Head and body = B and C (long and short stitch)
Highlights on head and body = F (long and short stitch)
Mane and tail = B and C (long and short stitch)
Ear = B and C (long and short stitch)
Hooves = D (satin stitch)
Mouth outline = D (split stitch)
Eye = G (granitos, straight stitch)

Saddle

Outline = H (stem stitch)
Saddle = E (long and short stitch)

Saddle blanket

Outline = H (stem stitch)
Scallops = F (satin stitch)

Rocker

Outer edge = E (stem stitch)
Highlight on outer edge = F (stem stitch, straight stitch)
Pink band = H (stem stitch)
Middle = F (stem stitch)
Rocker markings = N (2 strands, granitos)
Bridle and reins = A (stem stitch)

Roses

Centre = I (2 strands, 2 bullion knots, 10 wraps)
Inner petals = J (2 strands, 3 bullion knots, 16 wraps)
Outer petals = K (2 strands, 4 bullion knots, 16 wraps)

Rosebuds

Centre = I (2 strands, 1 or 2 bullion knots, 10 wraps)
Outer petals = J (2 strands, 2 bullion knots, 10 wraps)

Partial daisies = M (2 strands, detached chain)

Leaves = L (2 strands, detached chain)

Tiny buds = N (2 strands, French knot, 2 wraps)

GRENADIER GUARDS
by Susan O'Connor

Two dashing Grenadier Guards, resplendent in navy and scarlet, are the perfect touch for a child's bedroom or perhaps, a picture in a den.

This design uses
Couching, fly stitch, French knot, Ghiordes knot, satin stitch, stem stitch, straight stitch

Order of work

Guard

Satin stitch the jacket, working the sleeves then the body. Embroider the white belt, chest straps and gloves.

Work two sections of horizontal satin stitch for the trousers. Couch two strands of red yarn down the sides of the trousers to form the stripes.

Embroider the shoes and moustache using vertical satin stitches. Fill in the face around the moustache and then work a fly stitch around each glove for the outlines.

Add the chin strap and epaulettes with straight stitch and the buttons with French knots. The bearskin cap is stitched last. Beginning at the top, work horizontal rows of Ghiordes knots across the shape. Keep the loops approximately 10mm (⅜") long. Once the shape is completely filled, stand all the loops upright. Trim the loops evenly, leaving tufts approximately 6–8mm (¼–⁵⁄₁₆") long.

Commanding officer

Embroider the commanding officer in the same manner as the guard but add the gold regalia in stem and straight stitch after working the buttons. When stitching the bearskin cap, fill the area indicated on the pattern (*see page 124*) with red Ghiordes knots.

Requirements

Appletons 2 ply crewel wool
A = 202 ultra lt flame red
B = 448 dk orange red
C = 474 autumn yellow
D = 852 French navy blue
E = 965 iron grey
F = 991 white
G = 993 black
Wisper mohair nylon blend
H = W75 brown

Embroidery key

All embroidery is worked with two strands unless otherwise specified.

Bearskin cap on guard = G (Ghiordes knot)

Bearskin cap on commanding officer = B and G (Ghiordes knot)

Chin strap = C (straight stitch)

Face = A (1 strand, satin stitch)

Moustache on guard = H (satin stitch)

Moustache on commanding officer = E (satin stitch)

Jacket = B (satin stitch)

Belt and chest straps = F (satin stitch)

Buttons = C (French knot, 1 wrap)

Epaulettes = C (straight stitch)

Regalia on commanding officer = C (stem stitch, straight stitch)

Trousers = D (satin stitch)

Trouser stripes = B (couching)

Shoes = G (satin stitch)

Gloves = F (satin stitch)

Glove outlines = A (1 strand, fly stitch)

Toy Soldiers, Inspirations 13

FEATHERS
by Susan O'Connor

From softly shaded dove greys and whites to the rich tones of game birds and the vibrant colours of the rosella, these fabulous feathers are tantalisingly realistic.

These designs use
Encroaching stem stitch, long and short stitch, satin stitch, split stitch, stem stitch, straight stitch

Order of work

Feather 1

Stitch the quill and shaft from the base to the tip. Begin with encroaching stem stitch at the base and gradually change to stem stitch as the shaft becomes thinner.

Embroider the satin stitch sections, working the stitches for each half from the outer edge to the centre.

Feather 1

Feather 2

Beginning at the base, embroider the quill and shaft in the same manner as feather 1.

Stitch the upper section of the feather first, alternating the yarn colour for each marked segment to create the feather markings.

Work the soft downy feathers at the base, using split stitch for the longer feathers and straight stitch for the shorter ones.

Feather 3

Embroider the quill and shaft in stem stitch. Using the soft green yarn for most of the feather and the ecru yarn at the tip and base, stitch the feather in satin stitch.

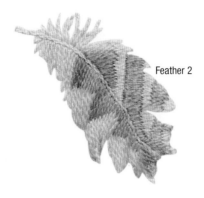
Feather 2

Feather 3

Feather 4

Work this feather in the same manner as feather 3, adding eleven straight stitches near the base to form the down.

Feather 4

Feather 5

Stitch the quill and shaft in encroaching stem stitch.

Using the powder blue yarn, work the satin stitch sections. Angle the stitches from the outer edge to the centre. Stitch four straight stitches extending from the feathers near the base. Next, embroider the down in the mint green yarn.

Feather 5

Feather 6

Embroider this feather in the same manner as feather 1, adding straight and split stitches to the base for down.

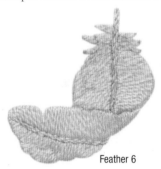
Feather 6

Feather 7

Embroider the quill with two lines of stem stitch worked side by side.

Outline the lower half of the feather and internal markings with long split stitches. Continue around the upper edge, adding the wispy ends with straight and split stitches.

Stitch the shaft in stem stitch. Fill in the feather with long and short stitch in the wider sections and satin stitch in the narrower sections.

Feather 7

Feather 8

Beginning with encroaching stem stitch at the base and gradually changing to stem stitch, embroider the ecru section of the quill. Using the grey yarn, work three split stitches alongside the first half of the quill. Change to the charcoal yarn and continue in stem stitch to the end of the quill. Beginning on the opposite side of the ecru stitching, embroider the shaft in stem stitch. Work the main part of the feather in satin stitch and long and short stitch. Add the ruffled ends to the feather with straight and split stitches. Fill in the spots with ecru satin stitches.

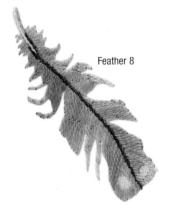

Feather 8

Feather 9

Stitch the ecru section of the quill in stem stitch. Change to the light tan yarn and work encroaching stem stitch next to the lower half of the ecru stitching. Embroider the shaft in stem stitch using the charcoal yarn.

Embroider the satin stitch sections, working the stitches for each half from the outer edge to the centre. Work the soft downy feathers at the base, using split stitch for the longer feathers and straight stitch for the shorter ones.

Feather 9

Feather 10

Beginning with encroaching stem stitch at the base and gradually changing to stem stitch, work the quill and shaft in the ecru yarn. Stitch three encroaching stem stitches in the medium tan yarn to complete the quill. Embroider the two charcoal stripes in satin stitch. Work the tan stripe between them in the same manner. Shading from the darkest colour near the stripes to the lightest near the quill, fill the remainder of the feather with long and short stitch.

Embroider the down at the base in satin stitch. Finally, add lines of tiny split stitches and stem stitches for the wisps at the sides.

Feather 10

Feather 11

Stitch the quill in encroaching stem stitch, gradually grading to stem stitch. Embroider the charcoal sections on either side of the quill in stem stitch. Continue working the shaft in encroaching stem stitch.

Embroider the satin stitch sections in the two grey yarns followed by the green satin stitched areas.

Finally, work the down near the base using straight stitches for the shorter pieces and split stitches for the longer pieces.

Feather 11

Feather 12

Embroider the quill of this rosella feather in encroaching stem stitch. Using the charcoal yarn and beginning part of the way along the upper side of the encroaching stem stitch, work the shaft in stem stitch. Work a small section of stem stitch on the lower side of the quill.

Stitch the blue sections of the feather, followed by the yellow and green sections. Finally, work the carlet sections.

Add straight stitches to the base of the feather for the shorter pieces of down and split stitches for the longer pieces.

The Feathers, Inspirations 20

Feather 12

110

Requirements

Gumnut Yarns 'Daisies' 1 ply crewel wool

A = 039 scarlet
B = 381 lt powder blue
C = 388 royal blue
D = 541 lt mint green
E = 584 lt bright green
F = 587 bright green
G = 624 soft green
H = 704 lemon
I = 708 sunflower yellow
J = 743 lt butter yellow
K = 744 butter yellow
L = 861 flesh pink
M = 865 shell pink
N = 867 dk shell pink
O = 941 ecru
P = 943 lt tan
Q = 945 med tan
R = 947 tan
S = 992 lt grey
T = 994 grey
U = 998 charcoal

Encroaching stem stitch

Encroaching stem stitch is a variation of stem stitch (see page 51) whereby the needle is angled across the line being stitched, rather than kept parallel to the line. This gives a wider looking stitch.

Embroidery key

All embroidery is worked with one strand.

Feather 1
Quill = O (encroaching stem stitch)
Shaft = O (stem stitch)
Feather = S (satin stitch)

Feather 2
Quill = O (encroaching stem stitch)
Shaft = O (stem stitch)
Feather = O and Q (satin stitch)
Down = O (straight stitch, split stitch)

Feather 3
Quill and shaft = O (stem stitch)
Feather = G (satin stitch)
Ends of feather = O (satin stitch)

Feather 4
Quill and shaft = O (stem stitch)
Feather = L (satin stitch)
Down = O (straight stitch)

Feather 5
Quill and shaft = O (encroaching stem stitch)
Feather = B (satin stitch, straight stitch)
Down = D (straight stitch, split stitch)

Feather 6
Quill = O (encroaching stem stitch)
Shaft = O (stem stitch)
Feather = J (satin stitch)
Down = K (straight stitch, split stitch)

Feather 7
Quill = O and G (stem stitch)
Shaft = N (stem stitch)
Internal markings = N (split stitch)
Outline = N (split stitch)
Feather = M (satin stitch, long and short stitch)
Wispy ends = N (straight stitch, split stitch)

Feather 8
Quill = O (encroaching stem stitch, stem stitch), T (split stitch)
Shaft = U (stem stitch)
Feather = T (satin stitch, long and short stitch)
Ruffled ends = T (straight stitch, split stitch)
Spots = O (satin stitch)

Feather 9
Quill = O (stem stitch), P (encroaching stem stitch)
Shaft = U (stem stitch)
Feather = R (satin stitch)
Down = R (straight stitch, split stitch)

Feather 10
Quill = O (encroaching stem stitch, stem stitch), Q (encroaching stem stitch)
Shaft = O (stem stitch)
Feather = O, P, Q and R (long and short stitch), Q, R and U (satin stitch)
Wispy ends = O and P (stem stitch, split stitch)

Feather 11
Quill = P (encroaching stem stitch, stem stitch)
Shaft = U (encroaching stem stitch)
Feather = G, S and T (satin stitch)
Down = S (straight stitch, split stitch)

Feather 12
Quill = P (encroaching stem stitch)
Shaft = U (stem stitch)
Feather = A, C, E, F and I (satin stitch)
Down = E, H and I (straight stitch, split stitch)

Patterns

Garland of
Spring Flowers
page 92

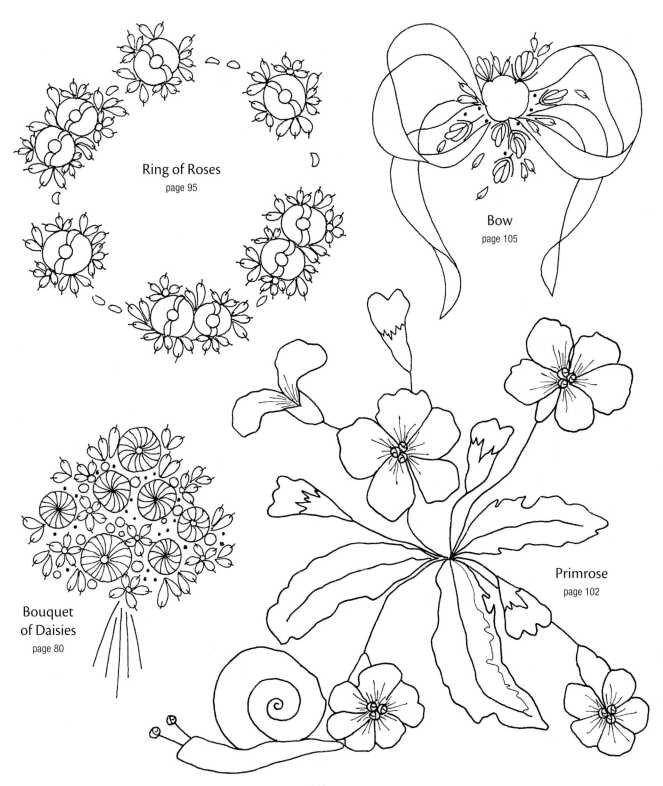

Ring of Roses
page 95

Bow
page 105

Bouquet
of Daisies
page 80

Primrose
page 102

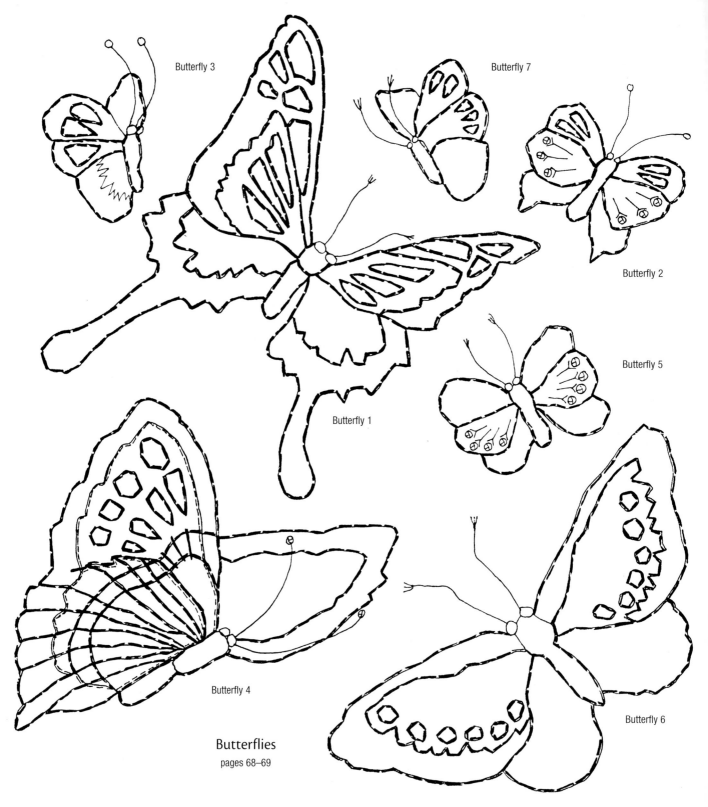

Butterfly 3

Butterfly 7

Butterfly 2

Butterfly 1

Butterfly 5

Butterfly 4

Butterfly 6

Butterflies
pages 68–69

Blue Wren
page 66

Chicken
page 63

Rabbit
page 72

stitch direction lines

Shasta Daisy
page 101

Basket
of Roses
page 74

Baby Birds
page 64

Bear
page 60

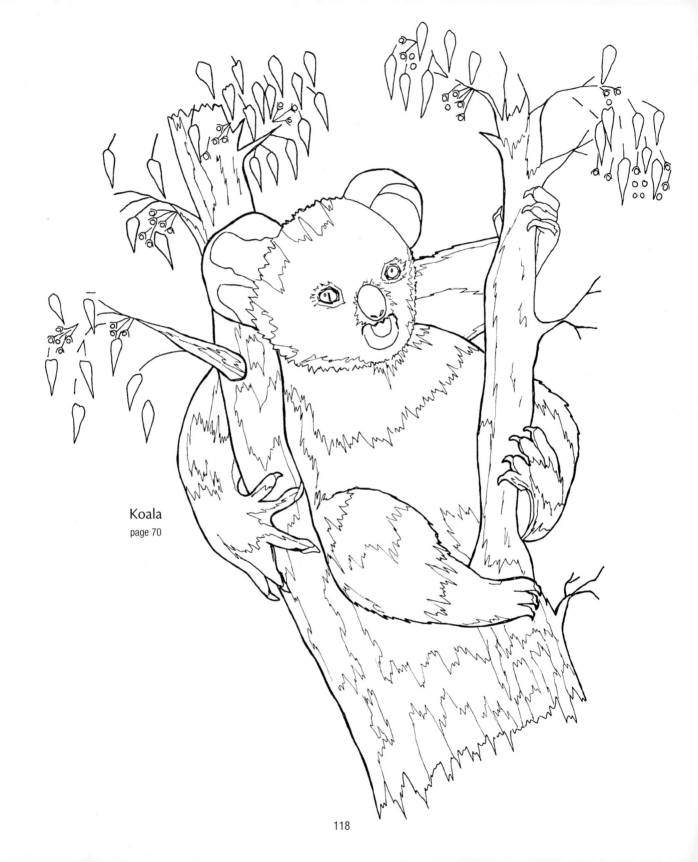

Koala
page 70

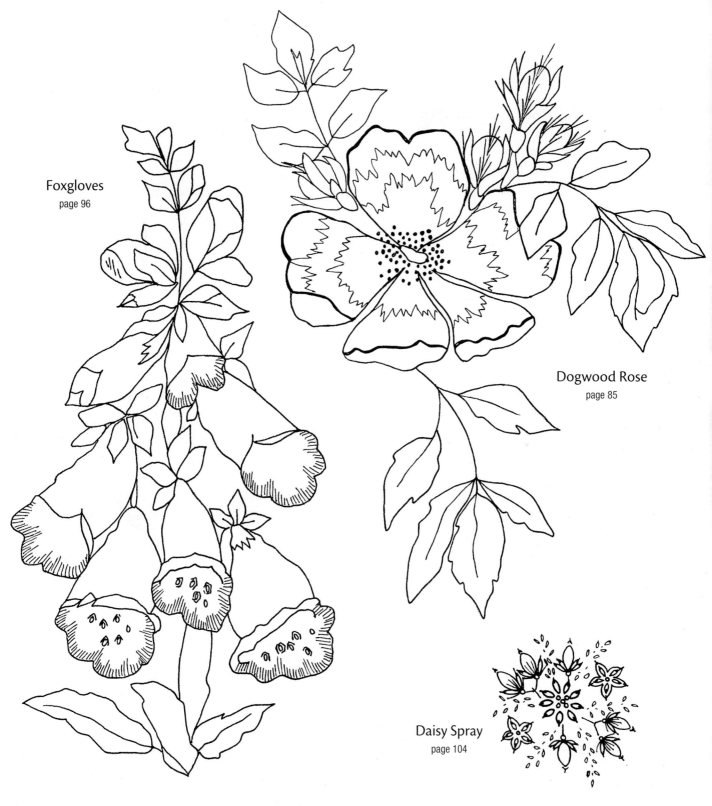

Foxgloves
page 96

Dogwood Rose
page 85

Daisy Spray
page 104

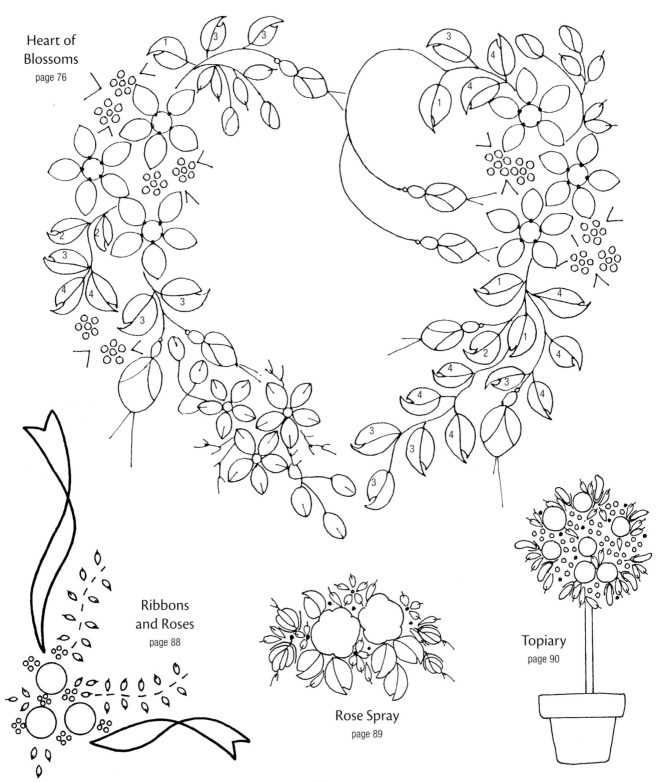

Heart of
Blossoms

page 76

Ribbons
and Roses

page 88

Rose Spray

page 89

Topiary

page 90

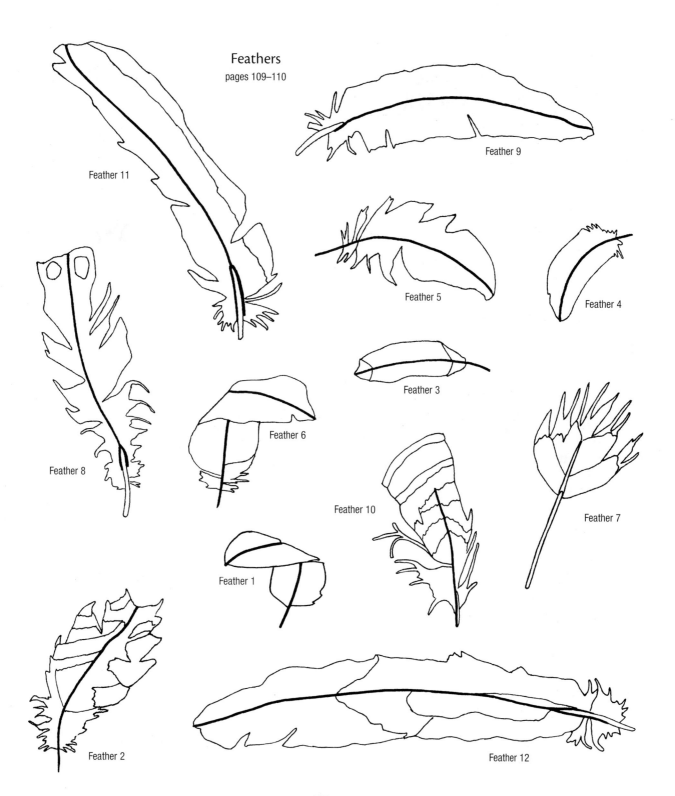

Feathers

pages 109–110

Feather 11

Feather 9

Feather 5

Feather 4

Feather 8

Feather 3

Feather 6

Feather 10

Feather 7

Feather 1

Feather 2

Feather 12

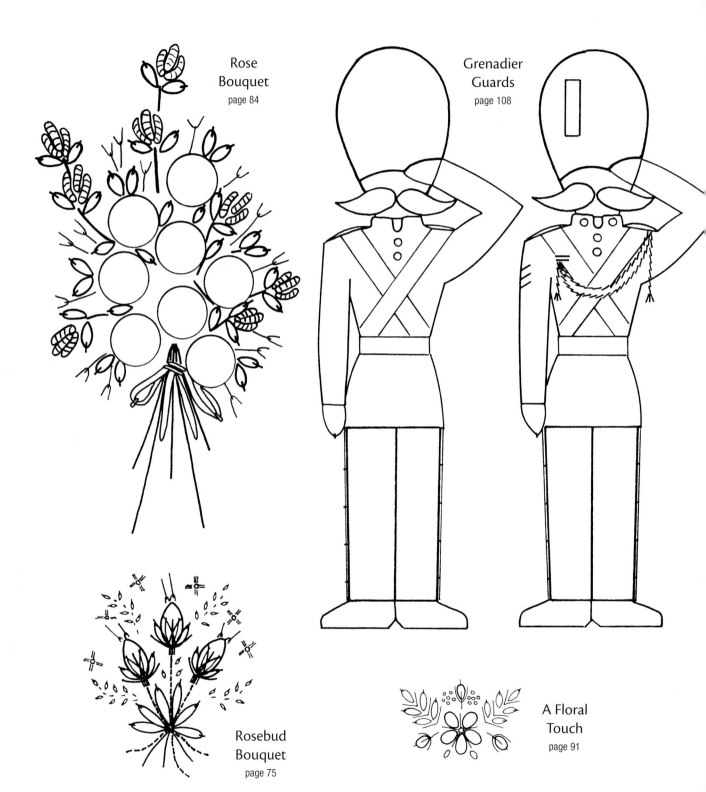

Rose
Bouquet
page 84

Grenadier
Guards
page 108

Rosebud
Bouquet
page 75

A Floral
Touch
page 91

Pansy
Bouquet
page 98

Jacobean
Circlet
page 86

1

2

2u

5u

3

4

5

6u

6

7

8u

8

9

Index

Italic numbers indicate pattern pages.

Acknowledgements

We are grateful to the talented embroiderers who have so readily shared their wonderful designs.

Margo Fanning, pages 64, 66, 85, 96, 101 and 102
Jean Harry, page 81
Annie Humphris, pages 75 and 104
Jan Kerton, page 91
Jenny McWhinney, pages 70 and 72
Susan O'Connor, pages 63, 68, 108 and 109
Margery Opie, page 86
Carolyn Pearce, pages 76, 92 and 98
Kris Richards, pages 74, 80, 89, 90, 95, 105 and 106
Bronwen Rossiter, page 84
Donna Stevens, page 88 *and*
Libby Vater, page 60.

First published in Great Britain 2017

Search Press Limited
Wellwood, North Farm Road,
Tunbridge Wells, Kent TN2 3DR

First published in Australia by Country Bumpkin Publications
© Country Bumpkin Publications

Photography by ADP

ISBN: 978-1-78221-180-8

The Publishers and author can accept no responsibility for any consequences arising from the information, advice or instructions given in this publication.

Suppliers
If you have difficulty in obtaining any of the materials and equipment mentioned in this book, then please visit the Search Press website for details of suppliers:
www.searchpress.com

Printed in China